Three Aspects of the Church

The Organization of the Church

BOOK 3

Witness Lee

Living Stream Ministry
Anaheim, CA • www.lsm.org

© 2007 Living Stream Ministry

All rights reserved. No part of this work may be reproduced or transmitted in any form or by any means—graphic, electronic, or mechanical, including photocopying, recording, or information storage and retrieval systems—without written permission from the publisher.

First Edition, December 2007.

ISBN 978-0-7363-3475-4

Published by

Living Stream Ministry
2431 W. La Palma Ave., Anaheim, CA 92801 U.S.A.
P. O. Box 2121, Anaheim, CA 92814 U.S.A.

Printed in the United States of America
07 08 09 10 11 12 13 / 9 8 7 6 5 4 3 2 1

CONTENTS

Title	Page
Preface	5
The Outline	7
1 Introduction	11
2 Principles concerning the Organization of the Church (1)	19
3 Principles concerning the Organization of the Church (2)	27
4 Principles concerning the Organization of the Church (3)	37
5 The Practice of the Organization of the Church (1)	47
6 The Practice of the Organization of the Church (2)	59
7 The Practice of the Organization of the Church (3)	69
8 The Practice of the Organization of the Church (4)	79
9 The Practice of the Organization of the Church (5)	85
10 The Practice of the Organization of the Church (6)	97
Supplementary Messages regarding Certain Matters in the Church That Require Our Attention	107
The Outline	109
1 There Being No Organizational Unification, among the Churches	111

2	Some Matters Related to Full-time Service (1)	121
3	Some Matters Related to Full-time Service (2)	133
4	Some Matters Related to Full-time Service (3)	143
5	Knowing the Spiritual Aspect of the Church (1)	149
6	Knowing the Spiritual Aspect of the Church (2)	161
7	Receiving People in the Churches	171
8	Fellowship Given in a Prayer Meeting concerning the Full-time Training	185

PREFACE

This book is composed of messages concerning the organization of the church given by Brother Witness Lee during a training on service in Taipei, Taiwan in 1956. The general subject of the training was "Three Aspects of the Church." The first aspect is the meaning of the church; the second, the course of the church; and the third, the organization of the church. The messages given in this training were compiled into three books, according to the three aforementioned aspects; these books are subtitled: *The Meaning of the Church, The Course of the Church,* and *The Organization of the Church.*

THE OUTLINE

I. Principles concerning the organization of the church:
   A. Being according to life.
   B. Being of the authority of God.
   C. Being according to function.
   D. Being according to ministry.
   E. Organization without life being a great mistake
   F. Those who serve properly always having the anointing.
   G. Samuel's anointing of David being the best example of a proper appointing of elders.
   H. Two kinds of submission to authority.
   I. Being according to order.
   J. All problems being the result of not keeping the order.
   K. A summary.
II. The practice of the organization of the church:
   A. The constituents of the church being God mingled with man and man mingled with God.
   B. The universal and local aspects of the church:
      1. The definition of these two aspects.
      2. The error of the Roman Catholic Church.
      3. The church not having a headquarters.
   C. The organization of the church having two aspects.
   D. The distinction between offices and gifts:
      1. The definition of offices and gifts.
      2. The importance of offices and gifts.
   E. Concerning offices:
      1. Apostles:
         a. Not being appointed by man.

      b. Being sent by God.
      c. The proof of apostleship being the fruit of an apostle's labor.
      d. Being one who submits to God's authority and who is sent by God.
      e. Proving an apostle:
        1) Apostles having the authority of God.
        2) Those who are under the work of an apostle needing to submit to his authority.
        3) To submit to an apostle's authority being to accept his apostleship.
    2. Elders and deacons:
      a. Those who appoint elders—the apostles who submit to the authority of the Holy Spirit.
      b. The qualifications of the elders and deacons:
        1) Submitting to the authority of the Holy Spirit.
        2) Experienced in life.
        3) Having functions.
      c. The appointment of elders and its relationship to the condition of the saints:
        1) There must be spiritual saints in order to have spiritual elders.
        2) For the glory and beauty of the church to be manifested, the apostles, elders, and saints all needing to be spiritual.
  F. Concerning gifts:
    1. The significance of gifts.
    2. Gifts being a matter of grace:
      a. The source of gifts being grace.
      b. The significance of grace.
    3. The two verses that speak of the relationship between gifts and grace:
      a. Two Scripture verses.
      b. Explanations of the two verses:
        1) Gifts being obtained according to grace.
        2) Gifts being sustained in grace.

4. Gifts being also a matter of life and of spirituality.
G. Conclusion.

Chapter One

INTRODUCTION

Scripture Reading: 1 Cor. 12:24, 27-30; Eph. 2:20-22

THE BIBLICAL VIEW CONCERNING THE ORGANIZATION OF THE CHURCH

Strictly speaking, the Bible does not use the phrase *the organization of the church*. This is because the church is not actually an organization. According to spiritual truth, it is wrong to say that the church is an organization. Nonetheless, due to the limitation of human understanding, it is necessary to use the term *organization* so that we can properly explain the church. Hence, according to spiritual fact, the church is not an organization, yet for the purpose of explanation and clarification, it seems necessary to use the term *organization*.

Although the church is not an organization, it is a living Body, an organism. Therefore, it has an aspect of organization. A body is an organism, an organic entity, whereas a table is not. A table is made by joining many individual pieces of wood together. It is merely an organization. On the other hand, our body is an organism. Nonetheless, it resembles an organization because outwardly speaking, our body has a structure composed of sinews, joints, blood, flesh, and other elements that have been joined together.

The Bible clearly reveals that the church is the Body of Christ (Eph. 1:22-23). Although a physical body looks like an organization, the most important characteristic of a body is not its organization but the life within. A mere organization has no life within. For example, both a table and a building are organizations. Regardless of size, they have no life within.

A body, on the contrary, is not a mere organization, because it has life within.

Since the church is the Body, its main characteristic is not organization but life. Once the life in a body stops functioning, it becomes a dead organization. To speak bluntly, when the life within a body is gone, what remains is merely a corpse, and a corpse is merely an organization. An organism depends on life. An entity that has life within is not only an organization but also an organism. An entity without life is merely an organization and has none of the activities related to life. The reason we say that the church is an organism is because it has life. The church is the Body of Christ.

In appearance both a physical body and the church seem to be organizations. However, just as a body is composed of different members, the church as an organism is composed of many living parts. An organism consists not merely of a single part but of many parts. If we speak of the Body of Christ without referring to our physical body, it will be difficult for us to understand the church. A body is a single organism, yet it has many parts, many constituents, which are mutually joined together. We cannot say that a body does not have organization; however, it is inaccurate to say that a body is merely an organization. The church is an organism with many parts and constituents coordinated and organized together.

Not only does the Bible say that the church is the Body; it also says that the church is a household, a temple of God, and the dwelling place of God (2:19-22). There is an aspect of organization in regard to a body and even more in regard to a house. A house is constructed of many parts and elements; hence, it is an organization. However, the church as a house is not a dead house but a living house. Every stone in a physical building is dead because stones lack life, but every stone in the church is living because these stones have life. First Peter 2:4-5 says, "Coming to Him, a living stone, rejected by men but with God chosen and precious, you yourselves also, as living stones, are being built up as a spiritual house." The Lord Himself is a living stone, and all of us saved ones are living stones. We are living stones because we have Christ's life in us. We are joined together not merely through outward coordination and arrangement but by inward union and growth in life.

Not only are a person's arms and shoulders connected together, but they also share the same life and the same circulation of blood. In other words, they are not only connected but have also grown together. Glass windows can be installed in a house, but the different parts of the church cannot be installed; instead, they grow together into the church. Nevertheless, we cannot deny the fact that the church has an aspect of organization.

Although the Bible does not use the word *organization*, it often uses related expressions. For instance, Matthew 16:18 uses the word *build*. The Lord wants to build His church on Himself as the rock. Ephesians 2:22 says that the saved ones are being built together into a dwelling place of God in spirit. Building is something organizational. Without being organized, big piles of wood and stone cannot become a building. After being organized, a piece of wood is located on top of another piece of wood, and a stone is located on top of another stone. This means that they are built. This is why we say that a building is something that involves organization.

Sometimes, when we go to a local church, we may sense that there is a heap of stones piled up. We may have the feeling that the brothers and sisters have not been built together. In other words, they have not passed through spiritual organization. When we visit another local church, we may sense that some of the brothers and sisters are being built together and have some spiritual organization. Others, however, may be like stones being piled up next to the house. They are for the building of the house, but they have not yet been built into the house. In other words, some saints in the church have not yet passed through spiritual organization.

Furthermore, even though the Bible does not speak of organization in relation to the church, it does speak of blending, or coordination. As to the church being a house, it is a building; as to the church being the Body, it is a blending. First Corinthians 12:24 speaks of the Body of Christ and uses our human body as a metaphor. It says, "God has blended the body together." Since this is a blending, or coordination, it certainly involves organization. God organizes everyone whom He blends together. When we come into the midst of some local churches, we cannot sense a condition of coordination; rather, we sense that what exists is a bunch of people coming together. They are not in confusion, but neither are they in coordination. This means that they have not been coordinated together, or organized, by God.

However, when we come into the midst of saints in another local church, we may sense their spiritual organization, that is, the blending carried out by God, and a beautiful order. This differs from a locality in which all the saints are scattered. In such a locality the saints may not argue or quarrel with one another but neither are they related to each other. Thus, *blending* is the spiritual term, whereas *organization* is the human term.

There is yet a third term that the Bible uses—*placed*. First Corinthians 12:28 says that what God has placed in the church is not merely one type of person but many types of people. Some are apostles, some are prophets, some are teachers, some are helpers, and some are administrators (v. 28). God has placed all these different types of people in the church. To use words that we can more easily understand, to be placed means to be organized. God's placing is His arrangement, and an arrangement is an organization. The gifted ones do not serve in a disorganized way, each doing his own thing. The apostles, prophets, and teachers do not serve independently. They do not speak their own thing. God's placing is orderly. In 1 Corinthians 12:28 there is a specific order. First there are apostles, second there are prophets, and third there are teachers. This is very orderly.

TWO ERRORS IN REGARD TO TWO EXTREMES

For the past two thousand years, Satan has done two kinds of work in regard to the organization of the church. On one hand, he replaces what is God-made with what is man-made, producing a well-ordered and hierarchical organization. The Roman Catholic Church today is the greatest hierarchical organization with the pope having nearly unlimited authority. When he gives a decree, all Catholics throughout the world need to obey. This is man-made. It is the same with today's Protestantism, which also has well-ordered, man-made hierarchical organizations. This is one aspect of Satan's work. The other aspect of Satan's work is to lead the believers to the opposite extreme, that is, away from well-ordered organization, whether man-made or God-made. Saints who claim to be delivered from the organization of Christianity may think that all believers are the same and are equal. This has some basis in the truth, but at the same time it is dangerous.

More than twenty years ago, when we were still young and had only recently been raised up by the Lord, we thought, due to the deep influence of Christianity, that all the saved ones were equal before God and that there was no need for any human arrangement or organization. In conducting our gospel meetings, we never arranged beforehand who would pray, who would speak, and who would be ushers. We made no arrangements at all. When the time arrived, everyone came together and sat in the meeting not knowing who was going to lead the singing, who was going to pray, and who was going to speak. We thought that all such arrangements belonged to man and that they were the product of human opinions and human organization; hence, we abandoned all these things. We forsook everything that was not clearly spoken of in the Bible. Hence, when we came together, we simply sat and waited for the leading and guiding of the Holy Spirit.

We cannot say that what we did then was wrong, but neither was it very prudent. Sometimes after we sat and waited for a while, we announced, "Today none of us has the leading of the Holy Spirit, so the meeting ends here. Since the Holy Spirit has not moved, we also should not move." This was the case with our Lord's table meeting, prayer meeting, fellowship meeting, gospel meeting, and edification meeting. When we came together, we simply sat and waited for the leading of the Holy Spirit. Even though we cannot say that we were wrong, we were too extreme.

According to the truth we are children of God and are equal; nevertheless, based on the order arranged by God, there is still a distinction. First Corinthians 12:28 says, "First apostles, second prophets, third teachers"; this is to have an order.

As children of God, we are all equal before God, but according to the order in the Body of Christ, we are not the same. For example, my head has the highest position in my body, and my feet occupy the lowest position in my body. They have entirely different positions. If my head and feet were in the same place, my body would be two-dimensional, not three-dimensional.

Every truth must be applied properly; otherwise, it can be taken to an extreme and become dangerous. While it is necessary to get rid of man-made hierarchal organizations, there is a need for a proper God-made and well-ordered placement to exist. We cannot deny that in the church God has an order of first, second, and third. Neither can we deny that the saints function as different parts of the Body. Some saints, in terms of their knowledge of God and what they have received from God and been entrusted with by God, are not that great; nevertheless, we cannot deny that each one has a particular function. The hands cannot say that the feet are not important and that every part should be a hand. Likewise, the feet cannot say that the hands are not important and that every part of the body should be a foot. The hands are the hands, and the feet are the feet. Each has its own function and functions accordingly.

The man-made organization within Catholicism and Protestantism surely offends God. I speak this word not as a criticism of others but as a warning to ourselves. However, if we think that all the saints are the same and are equal, this too is erroneous and unscriptural. Hence, we should not be intolerant when we hear the word *organization*. On one hand, the church is not an organization; on the other hand, the church is not completely without organization. God has placed some in the church in the position of first, second, third, and so forth. Some people may say that this order is only for explanation and that it is not an actual order. However, if this were the case, why did God not first speak of the interpretation of tongues and then of the apostles? The order in which they are presented is in fact an order. In the church the apostles are ranked first.

As an illustration, the New Testament always places apostles and prophets together, but it never says, "Prophets and apostles." Rather, it always says, "Apostles and prophets" (Eph. 3:5; 4:11). This is the order in the Bible. Ephesians 2 says that we are "being built upon the foundation of the apostles and prophets" (v. 20). This proves that in the church there is a distinction of order according to God's placing. This placing, in human words, is organization. A placing is an arrangement, and since it is an arrangement, it cannot be separated from the term *organization*.

It is a fact that the church has organization, but this fact should never be separated from life. The church is not merely an organization but an organism, an entity that has life within. We should not deny the fact that the church has organization, yet we should recognize that the church is truly an organism, an organic entity. The reason that we use the term *organization* is for the purpose of expressing and explaining an aspect of the church. However, we should never confuse our usage of the term and think that we are referring to an organization like that which exists in Catholicism and Protestantism and from which we have been delivered.

THE REASON FOR USING THE TERM *ORGANIZATION* AND THE NECESSARY PRECAUTION RELATED TO USING THIS TERM

We cannot avoid using the term *organization,* because even the word *coordination* sometimes cannot convey the full meaning of what we are trying to describe. Nevertheless, we must be cautious in using this term and not consider the church to be merely an organization. We must remember that the church has life within. Throughout the past two thousand years, many organizations within the church have not been according to biblical principles and have even offended the Holy Spirit. As a result, many godly people condemn the usage of the word *organization*. However, we should not avoid using this term because of its previous misuse; rather, we should consider the organization of the church according to the principles found in the Scriptures and in relation to the authority of the Holy Spirit.

CHAPTER TWO

PRINCIPLES CONCERNING THE ORGANIZATION OF THE CHURCH

(1)

BEING ACCORDING TO LIFE

The organization of the church is a matter of growth. Whether we speak of the church as the Body or as a house, both are the issue of growth. This is because the organization of the Body is of life, and the organization of the church as a house is also of life. As a house, it is the growing together of living stones. The church is not without organization. It absolutely has organization, but its organization is of life. We cannot study this matter according to reason; rather, we need to prove and test it according to life.

Let us suppose that a brother becomes an elder. His being an elder is definitely something related to organization; otherwise, it would be unlawful and illegal. The raising up and the appointment of an elder in the church is a matter of spiritual organization. If a brother becomes an elder but cannot supply life to others nor receive the life supply from others, his being an elder is merely a matter of man-made organization. However, if his being an elder is an issue of the growth in life, he will be able to supply life to others and also receive the supply of life from others. Hence, the organizational fact related to his being an elder is based on the inward reality of life. Based simply on outward appearance, it is inaccurate to say that having elders is organizational and that such organization is wrong.

In the past, among the churches in different places in mainland China, some elders were elders purely in an organizational sense. Whenever we thought of their serving as elders, we had an inward sense of death. Whenever we observed them handling church affairs, we sensed death. With them there was no supply of life. Their being made elders was purely a matter of outward organization. In principle this was Catholicism and Protestantism. It was not the work of the Holy Spirit. An elder who is an elder among the saints according to the arrangement of the Holy Spirit will produce in people a sense of life. They will sense life in his person and in his carrying out of his office, that is, in the carrying out of his duty and position as an elder. If an elder is merely an elder according to an outward arrangement in the way of organization and not as the result of growth in life, he himself will sense that there is no life in his eldership. He will sense that his eldership is dead, not living.

The church is not without organization. On the contrary, the church has organization, yet this organization is of life. The organization of the church is of life just as the organization of a body is of life. The church is an organism. All those who work for the Lord need to be careful. They should not think that they can appoint elders, deacons, and other serving ones merely according to the Bible. This matter is not so simple. In principle, one who is sent by the Lord for His work is an apostle, and as such, he may appoint elders in the churches. However, if the appointment of elders is based merely on this principle, it will be only a matter of human organization carried out according to dead regulations and in letter. It will be no different from the dead situation found in Protestantism. All those who work for the Lord must seek the Lord cautiously and seriously in regard to their appointing of elders and choosing of deacons. They need to ask, "Will this brother be an elder who will be able to supply life to the saints? Will he be able to dispense life to the church? Moreover, will he be able to receive the supply of life from the church?" This is an accurate test.

Every elder must also examine himself before God in a serious way. He must ask, "Today, am I, as an elder serving and administrating in the church, able to touch the life supply? Am I able to render a life supply?" If an elder's answer to these questions is in the negative, he is in the wrong position. If a member of a body is in the proper position, there will be the circulation of blood within him, and he will be able to supply blood to others and receive a supply of blood from others. We can be clear regarding whether our position is proper or not, based upon whether our inner being is living and has the sense of being alive.

There should be no competition in the matter of service. For example, a brother may have been saved for fifteen years, whereas another brother, who has an important position in the church, may have been saved for only fourteen years. The brother who was saved a year earlier should not expect to be in the same position simply because he has been saved longer. This is not proper.

We must know that our place in the church is something of life and is an issue of the growth in life. If we try to compete with others and seek to be in their position, the result will be death. For example, if a brother stands up to speak and does not keep his place in his speaking, those listening to him will feel uneasy and uncomfortable within, even though they cannot explain why. This is because his speaking is not according to the Spirit. This situation produces death, not life, and it is not the issue of the growth in life.

Is a certain arrangement in the service proper? Should certain ones serve as deacons? Should a certain brother be responsible to take the lead in a service? All these questions cannot be determined outwardly but must pass through a strict test. Being an elder, a deacon, or a responsible one for a home meeting or a small group is a matter that should be tested before God. Competition or comparison with others does not matter. The only way is to submit under the Head. This is the way to receive mercy and grace.

If a brother is appointed to be an elder or a deacon, our response should be to tell the Lord, "O Lord, praise You for appointing and using my brother. Even though he is younger than I, even though I have been saved for ten years and he for only four years, I worship You. You are the Head. I am a member." This is the way to be blessed. In the church we should not make comparisons or engage in competition. It is God who appoints, and it is Christ who builds. All the matters in the church are of life and are not controlled by human hands.

Anything that is of life is beyond human manipulation. If there is really life, there is life. If there is no life, there simply is no life. If the activities of the saints in their service in the church are in life, everyone will sense it; however, if their service is not carried out in life, everyone will also sense this. Not only will everyone else sense it, but even the ones not serving in life will sense it. The saints can sense whether they are serving in life or in competition with others.

If the children of God do not serve and coordinate in life, they will compare, and even more seriously, they will compete. God's children should not neglect life, simply because the church has organization. Once they neglect life, the church will no longer be an organism. It will be a dead entity. This is terrible. Those of us who work for the Lord should be careful; we must not stretch out our hands to appoint people in a careless manner. We cannot and should not do this. Let us suppose that a co-worker says, "I am a worker; why can I not appoint elders?" Such a word demonstrates that he is not qualified to appoint elders. His word is a proof that he is not in life. Being an elder is a matter of growth in life, and even the appointment of elders has to be of life. Not only in the appointing of elders, but even in the appointing of deacons and those responsible for small groups, the brothers need to be careful to always check whether or not they are touching life or touching death and whether their appointment is of life or merely of organization. This is a solemn matter.

We should have coordination and arrangement among us; that is, we should have organization. However, what we have should not be mere coordination, arrangement, or organization. It should be the issue of growth in life. When we appoint elders and deacons, we should bow our heads and worship the Lord, saying, "Lord, there are a few brothers in the church who have grown. It is Your abundant life that has produced these elders and deacons. Lord, we worship You." How sweet this is!

Strictly speaking, those who cannot and do not know how to touch the sense of life are not qualified nor worthy to appoint elders. It is dangerous if they do so; hence, they should never attempt to touch this matter. We should never think that we are the one to take care of a messy situation simply because no one else is taking care of it. We must know that unless it is of life, our taking care of such a situation will be similar to Uzzah and the Ark of God in 2 Samuel 6:1-7. The result will be death. The important matter is not whether the condition is messy, but whether we have touched life inwardly in our service, arrangement, and coordination. We must use life as the test. The church definitely has coordination, arrangement, and organization, but all these matters must be in life.

BEING OF THE AUTHORITY OF GOD

The organization of the church issues from the growth in life, and the arrangement in the organization is altogether a matter of the authority of God. In the church the authority of God is the Holy Spirit. All the arrangement in our serving should be tested by life and by the authority of God—the Holy Spirit. When a brother is appointed to be an elder, those appointing him should ask, "Is the authority of the Holy Spirit in this brother? Does the Holy Spirit reign in the matter of his being made an elder? Is there the authority of God in this appointment or arrangement? Does this appointment issue from the authority of man or from the authority of the Holy Spirit?"

God has sometimes given me a commission to appoint elders in a locality. At such times, what I fear the most is that I might exercise my authority and offend God's authority. I am not afraid of making a wrong arrangement; I am afraid that the arrangement might come out of my authority and not out of God's authority. We are able to realize and sense such matters; hence, we need to be cautious.

The organization of the church is a matter of life and of authority. Who is ruling? Is it man, or is it the Holy Spirit? Is it us, or is it God? This is a solemn matter. If man rules, this is according to the principle of the Roman Catholic Church. The Holy Spirit must rule, and the authority must be in the hands of the Holy Spirit. Only then can we be the church. Hence, we who work for the Lord and serve in various places must check with ourselves concerning where the authority for our coordination lies. Not only should the leading brothers ask themselves concerning who has the authority, but also those who are learning to serve should ask themselves whether in obeying the leading brothers they are obeying man or obeying God. If they are merely obeying man and man's authority, their obedience is wrong.

In the organization and coordination of the church, not only should those who serve as authorities be careful about the matter of authority, but also those who submit to them need to take heed to this matter. If a brother is elderly and is a deputy authority, he needs to ask himself whether it is he or the Holy Spirit who has the authority. As those who submit to authority, the saints also need to check whether they are submitting to man's authority or God's authority. This is not difficult. Every saint can sense this. If a saint submits to the authority of the Holy Spirit, inwardly he will sense the supply of life; however, if he submits to man's authority, he will immediately sense that he is detached from the Body and that he is dead. Every saint has the capacity to discern this.

I hope that all the saints will realize that in the organization of the church there is the matter of the authority of God. If someone submits to my authority because of who I am, or if I submit to others' authority because of who they are, it is wrong. The significance of being an authority and submitting to an authority is related to the authority of God. Why should I submit to a certain brother? It is because I recognize that he has the authority of God. I have been shown mercy and have learned the lesson that there is an order and a building in the church. I know that God has placed brothers above me, and I have nothing to say. This kind of submission to authority has enabled me to touch life, the presence of God, and the fellowship of the Spirit.

There is another kind of submission that gives us a sense of death. This is something of Babylon, not of the New Jerusalem or the church. There is organization in the church, but every item and aspect of this organization issues from God's authority. Those who serve as authorities are under God's authority, and those who submit to authority are also under

God's authority. The submission of some of the brothers and sisters among us still bears the flavor of society; it is the submission common in a human community and is not a result of seeing the authority of God.

In arranging the services, the responsible brothers in the church need to be able to tell the Lord, "O Lord, this arrangement issues altogether from Your authority." Only this is proper. Many times even though the brothers may agree among themselves, their inner feeling does not agree with them. In appointing elders, the co-workers especially need to examine and touch the Lord's feeling with a clean conscience, just as Samuel did when he anointed David (1 Sam. 16:1-13). Our inward motive must be that we are but a messenger and that the authority is in God's hands. We must allow God to reign in every appointment. Moreover, everyone who is appointed must know God's authority and realize that he is not submitting to man's authority but to God's authority, to the Head of the church. This bears an entirely different flavor.

The organization of the church must be of life. Although there are arrangements and coordination, these must issue from the inward growth in life because the church is the Body of Christ, an organism. The organization of the church must also be under the authority of God. The arrangements and coordination must be the result of God's authority, of the authority of the Holy Spirit, not the issue of man's authority.

CHAPTER THREE

PRINCIPLES CONCERNING THE ORGANIZATION OF THE CHURCH

(2)

The organization of the church must be according to the life and authority of God. Moreover, the organization of the church must also be according to function and ministry.

BEING ACCORDING TO FUNCTION

Although there is such a thing as place or position in the organization of the church, our emphasis should be function, not position. We should not bring the thought of position into the church; rather, we must emphasize the matter of function. The elders in a church do not have a higher position than the other brothers and sisters; rather, the elders carry more weight in regard to function. For example, in a local church it is less serious for the general condition of the brothers and sisters to be poor than for the function of the elders to be poor. If the function of the elders is poor, the church will suffer much loss. We need to respect the elders because their function in the church is of great importance.

When elders, deacons, and responsible ones are appointed and designated for specific services, it must be done according to life, in submission to the authority of the Holy Spirit, and according to function. We need to ask, "How much function will this brother have as an elder or a deacon?" Some who have been appointed as elders are like the deaf; they cannot hear the voice of the Holy Spirit. Others are like the blind; they cannot see the work of the Holy Spirit. Whereas life has to be recognized through experience, function can be more readily discerned by considering a person's place in the church, the coordination he is involved in, and what his particular portion is. Inwardly, these are matters of life, and outwardly, they are matters of function. Many other things can be hidden from others, but a person's function is not something that can be hidden.

At this point we want to make a distinction between gifts and function. Many people have gifts, but they may not function. It is not easy for a person without a gift to function, but often, gifted people do not have much function in the church. For example, a sister may be able to play the piano well; hence, this is her gift. Nevertheless, she may not function in the church because of a bad temper and poor character. When she is angry, she simply walks out of a meeting. Moreover, she may not pay attention to the time and often arrives late. Although a meeting may start at a certain time in the evening, she may arrive ten minutes late, when the singing has stopped. Although she plays the piano very well, she has no function in the church.

Some people are not without gifts, but their gifts are superficial. For example, the Old Testament gives an account of a donkey that was able to speak human language (Num. 22:21-30). This surely was a gift. The New Testament makes mention of people speaking in tongues and being able to heal the sick, both of which are gifts (1 Cor. 12:9-10). However, having gifts does not necessarily mean that one is able to function. Gifts are superficial and simple, but to function properly is not. If a person wants to be useful, to function, he needs many things in addition to a gift. For example, a certain brother in a local church may truly have the gifts necessary to be an elder, but his function may be spoiled by a bad temper. In other words, although he has the gifts, due to his bad temper, he may not have the function of an elder. Therefore, functions are greater than gifts. To function requires more than possessing a gift.

Some might then ask, "Do gifts plus life issue in function?" Gifts plus life may not necessarily issue in function. This is because function is very much related to a person's character. Even though a person may have a gift and a certain amount of life, he may not have a function. In order to function, he must have God's life wrought into him to the extent that a proper character is produced within him. For example, a brother may have a gift related to preaching the gospel, but he may lack perseverance. When he preaches the gospel in a certain place, if there are no results after three or five days or no one is saved after a month, he will give up. Likewise, another brother may be satisfied with a small result and quit preaching. Both are short of perseverance. Perseverance is missing in their character.

Perseverance is related to endurance. Some brothers have the gift of teaching and are able to shepherd and teach people, but they lack endurance. They are able to give good messages, but because they lack endurance, they do not function much. Suppose there are two brothers who both have a gift for preaching the gospel, the first one being more gifted than the second one. It may be that the function of the second is greater than that of the first. After the first one lives in a certain place for a year, he may not be able to continue in the work of the gospel. Although he has a greater gift, due to his lack of endurance, he is not able to continue to labor for more than a year. However, the work of the second one, who is not as gifted but has endurance, will begin to flourish once he has been in a certain place for more than a year. Hence, a person with a greater gift may not necessarily have a greater function. His gift must be matched with the proper character in order for him to have a corresponding function.

Character refers to the way we are. We must allow the life of God to change the way we are. Our lazy character and sloppy disposition must be dealt with by God's life. If a person is short of perseverance, always expecting to accomplish a task instantly, his disposition, his way of being, must be transformed by God's life. If a person has no endurance, is not able to accommodate others, and handles matters in a sloppy manner, his temperament must be dealt with by God's life. Although he may be gifted, his laziness, sloppiness, carelessness, and lack of perseverance and endurance will cause him to have no function.

We have seen many gifted brothers and sisters in the

church whose functions are not manifested because of their poor character. This is pitiful. Moreover, if elders, deacons, and responsible ones are appointed based merely upon gift and not function, the appointed ones will be a trouble to the church in the future. Those who are gifted but without function are dangerous in the church and will eventually harm the church. I hope that the young brothers and sisters will pay special attention to this matter, that is, that they would not focus merely on gift and neglect function. If they do this, they will be dangerous persons in the church. Having a gift does not require the Lord's dealing, but functioning absolutely requires His dealing. A person whose function is manifested among the saints and in the church must be one who has been dealt with. Such a one may be an elder without much gift, but he definitely has a portion, a function, in the eldership.

Function includes gift, but gift does not include function. Function is gift plus something more. Function is gift matched with character. Some people are gifted, but their person is short. In other words, their character does not match their gift. If they want their character to match their gift, they must pass through the cross and experience the life of Christ. The lessons that the Lord's life leads us to learn are very practical. To speak inaccurately or do things in a sloppy manner proves that one has not learned the lessons taught by the Lord's life. In other words, if a person has learned the lessons related to life and the cross, he will be serious and strict in doing things and will speak accurately.

A person who has passed through the cross and been worked on by Christ's life will not be lazy and sloppy. He will not come to a meeting late. To do otherwise, indicates that one has not learned the lessons taught by the Lord's life.

Gifts do not have much to do with life, but to function requires that one learn the lessons related to life. The more strongly a person experiences the dealing of the cross and the deeper he experiences the work of Christ's life, the more his function will be manifested. If a co-worker appoints an elder or a deacon according to the brother's function, the result will be very positive; however, if he ignores a person's function and focuses on his gift, the result will be unthinkable.

If a worker of the Lord appoints elders or deacons merely according to their ability to handle matters and deliver spoken messages, stressing gifts more than function, the result will be that the whole church will experience death. Such an appointment is not according to the Holy Spirit or life, and it is not produced organically. Gifts are not sufficient to serve as the basis of one's service. A person's service in the church should be determined not according to his gift but according to his function. The amount of function and the kind of function a brother has determine what portion he should have in the service. Without a certain function, he cannot serve in a certain capacity, nor can he have a corresponding portion in the service. Those who work for the Lord must hold firmly to this principle.

Gifts are not produced by life but are something added outwardly. Functions are produced by the inward growth in life. To function requires that we conduct ourselves properly as befitting men. Our character should be that of behaving in a manner that befits a proper man. This requires that we experience the dealing of the cross and the inward working of Christ's life. Our function in the church is the result of matching our character, which has been dealt with by the cross and worked on by Christ's life, to a gift. Ninety percent of our function in the church depends upon our character, and only ten percent depends upon our gift. However, the character of which I speak is not our natural character. Our natural character is worthless. Our character is valuable only when it has been dealt with by the cross and been worked on by the resurrection life.

Our natural meekness, perseverance, endurance, and reverence are worthless in the church. However, after we have been dealt with by the cross and have experienced the resurrection life, we will have in the Lord the virtues of meekness, perseverance, and endurance. Moreover, we will fear God and be earnest in whatever we do. This kind of character is the main constituent of a proper function. If we are such a person, it does not matter whether our gift is small. As long as we remain in the church year after year, our function will spontaneously be manifested. If a church is committed into our hand, after a period of time it will be built up. Once the Lord has worked on our character, we will have a particular portion and function.

BEING ACCORDING TO MINISTRY

The organization of the church must be according to life and according to the authority of God; moreover, it must also be according to function and ministry. The distinction between function and ministry is that function is general, whereas ministry is specific. Of course, whoever has a ministry has a function. Conversely, everyone who has a function has a ministry. For example, in Acts 6 Stephen was among those who served tables. His serving tables was a ministry (vv. 2-3, 5). However, we are speaking of ministry in a higher and larger sense. We are speaking of ministry in the sense of Paul's ministry (Rom. 11:13; 2 Cor. 4:1).

The general coordination in the church is according to function; the specific coordination in the church is according to ministry. Apostles, prophets, evangelists, and shepherds and teachers (Eph. 4:11) all have particular ministries. They do not merely have particular functions, as do all brothers and sisters. They also have particular ministries. Generally speaking, all brothers and sisters have respective functions; however, in the church some also have particular ministries, specific ministries. Ministry involves a higher requirement than function.

When we speak of function and ministry, we must set aside the matter of gifts. When we speak of the coordination in the church, we must set aside the matter of gifts because gifts are dangerous. If the appointment of elders and deacons in a local church is based upon gift, the church will suffer loss. Appointments should be made not according to gifts but according to function. Function has certain requirements, whereas gifts do not. Nevertheless, the requirements for ministry are even higher than that for function. The requirements for having a function are general, whereas the requirements for having a ministry are specific.

The ministry of a person who serves God is produced through the specific work of God on that person. Once God has worked on a person to a certain extent, He produces a ministry within that person. Madame Guyon is an excellent example. Although she went to be with the Lord many years ago, her life story has continued to render immeasurable help to many who have come after her. This immeasurable help is due to the ministry formed within her. The help she has rendered to the church and the supply she has rendered to the saints come out from her ministry. Her ministry was produced through God's work in her over a prolonged period of time.

Gift plus character equals function. This means that a gift plus a certain degree of growth in life, that is, learning the lessons of life, equals function. However, the requirement of ministry is even higher. To have a ministry requires us to pass through a considerably long process in God's hand in regard to certain matters and certain aspects. For instance, Paul had a ministry. On the one hand, he was a minister, and on the other hand, he had a ministry. The words *minister* and *ministry* are both used in 2 Corinthians 3. *Ministers* in verse 6 refers to persons, whereas *ministry* in verses 8 through 9 refers to a service. Paul, a minister with a ministry, surely passed through a great deal of God's work. Such a ministry could not have been produced in a short period of time or through a few shallow experiences.

For a person to have a ministry in the church requires that he be deep in the Lord, having passed through a great deal of God's constituting work, and having been dealt with by God to a great extent. Every person who becomes an apostle must have acquired a certain amount of spiritual constitution by passing through many dealings in God's hand. Only such a person can be constituted with a ministry. If a person does not have a ministry, he should not be considered as an apostle. Not all those who serve the Lord are apostles. All those who serve the Lord should ask themselves, "As one serving the Lord, do I have a ministry?" In the Bible the apostles spoke clearly concerning their respective and distinctive ministries (Rom. 11:13; Acts 1:17; 20:24; 2 Cor. 4:1). Peter, James, John, and Paul each had a ministry.

In the coordination, or organization, of the church, we need to pay attention to life and to the authority of God. We also need to pay attention to function and to ministry. If we do not pay attention to these basic issues, we will always encounter problems in our coordination. Although a brother has been sent by the Lord to serve the Lord, if others do not perceive the ministry in him and receive help from him, he cannot be called an apostle. An apostle is a person with a ministry; that is, he is a person who has been dealt with by God and constituted with God. As a result, others will be able to see that he has the measure of an apostle and realize that he has a portion that the church needs. As such, he is not a person who can easily be dispensed with in the church. In other words, after having passed through a certain amount of God's work, he has gained a portion of ministry that is indispensable in the church.

The Bible shows that Paul, Peter, and James each had their particular portion in the ministry. Such portions are not gifts but ministries. According to the Bible, every member in the Body of Christ has a ministry. Even the smallest member has a ministry and a function. It is difficult to separate ministry from function, although experientially there is a distinction between them.

A number of brothers among us consider that since they serve the Lord and have been sent by the Lord, they can act as if they are apostles who are able to do certain things in the church. To have such an attitude and intention is wrong. This is to take the way of the Roman Catholic Church. In the Roman Catholic Church a person acquires a position when he becomes a priest. However, it is not so among us. If we serve the Lord full time, we should not think that we have acquired a special position because we are a worker of the Lord. A person's measure in the church depends upon his spiritual ministry and spiritual constitution. The organization of the church depends on life, the authority of God, function, and ministry. It is wrong to be in a certain position without having a certain ministry, just as it is wrong to be in a certain position without a corresponding function.

In regard to the organization of the church, we should pay attention to four items—life, authority, function, and ministry. As an organism, the church must pay attention to these four items. If any of these four items are missing, there will be problems. When we observe the condition of a local church, we need to consider the condition of the items of life, authority, function, and ministry in the coordination of the saints. If all of these four items are in a proper condition, the result will be a wonderful, living, and healthy organism, a church under the authority of the Holy Spirit. If this is not the case, the result will be that the church will have problems and be in a sick condition.

I hope that among us no one will oppose the use of the expression *the organization of the church*. I also hope that no one would consider that since there is organization in the church, he can arrange and coordinate according to his preference. This should never be done. All the arrangements and coordination should be according to life, authority, function, and ministry. Without these four items, no one should discuss any arrangement or matter of coordination. This is a solemn matter.

What a beautiful sight it would be if all the brothers who are elders would grow in life, be subject to the authority of the Holy Spirit, bear the mark of having been passed through and dealt with by God, allow the cross and Christ's life to deal with and work on their character, have the authority of God, function, and bear their responsibility as elders.

In the past, in some local churches the matter of appointing elders was carried out in an improper way. Some who were called by the Lord forsook their jobs and began to serve the Lord full time; however, because they were called by the Lord to work for the Lord, they considered themselves to be apostles with the ability to appoint elders. This is a wrong concept. This is not what is spoken of in *The Normal Christian Church Life*. According to the letter, this may seem to be correct, but it is a wrong application of the truth. For a person to be able to appoint elders in the churches requires that God work on him to a great extent. If a full-time serving one has only recently been called by the Lord to serve the Lord full time, it is wrong to say that he can appoint elders.

Those who serve in the church should not apply these words to others. Every elder, deacon, and responsible one must check with himself, especially the brothers and sisters who serve full time, asking, "Have I assumed the position of a worker for myself? In the arrangement and coordination in the church, what is my condition in life, what is my relationship to the authority of the Holy Spirit, and what is my function and ministry?" If we disregard these questions, we will become a dead organization. A dead organization does not have the life of God, the authority of the Holy Spirit, the functions that are according to the Lord's dealing, and a ministry constituted of the Holy Spirit. A dead organization has only dead arrangement and lifeless coordination.

When we speak concerning the organization of the church, we need to pay attention not only to the truth in the New Testament but also to our actual situation. We realize that this matter is solemn because we have seen the danger; that is, we have seen that if we are not cautious and serious in taking care of this matter, we will become a dead organization in which there is no life of God, no authority of the Holy Spirit, no function that is according to the Lord's dealing, and no ministry that has been constituted of the Holy Spirit. We do not want to correct these mistakes with our human hand, but we look to the Spirit of God to work in each of our hearts. I hope that all of us would humbly submit ourselves under the hand of the Holy Spirit.

We should not be proud, and we should not despise others. We all need the Lord's grace in order to come back to the Lord and ask Him, "O Lord, do I exercise my portion properly in the church?" We all must endeavor to do one thing; that is, we must allow the Holy Spirit to have the authority among us. We cannot deny that there is an order in the church; nevertheless, we must be fearful so that this order would be according to life, the Lord's authority, function, and ministry. May the Lord have mercy on us so that we would be on the alert and would not allow the church to fall into the condition of a dead organization. For this, we must pay attention to four items—life, authority, function, and ministry.

CHAPTER FOUR

PRINCIPLES CONCERNING THE ORGANIZATION OF THE CHURCH

(3)

ORGANIZATION WITHOUT LIFE BEING A GREAT MISTAKE

There is organization in the church, but this organization must be according to the life of God. When we speak of coordination and service in the church, we cannot avoid using the term *organization*. In every local church there is an order, an arrangement, related to the elders, deacons, and serving ones. This obviously involves organization; we cannot deny this. However, we must pay attention to the fact that this organization must have life as its content. To have organization without life is a great mistake.

We are reluctant to use the term *organization* in order to avoid causing the church to fall into a state in which there is only organization but not the inner life. Christianity has been in error for two thousand years because it has many different organizations that are contrary to biblical principles. These organizations limit the freedom of the Holy Spirit and greatly contradict the work of the Holy Spirit. For this reason, many godly people condemn the matter of organization. On our part, although the word *organization* has negative connotations, we do not categorically refuse to use it. Nevertheless, when we use this term, we must be careful to avoid the error of organization in its unscriptural sense, a sense that limits and contradicts the Holy Spirit.

THOSE WHO SERVE PROPERLY ALWAYS HAVING THE ANOINTING

When a person is serving, he will have a sense within. If

his service is of life, he will sense the anointing and the supply of life while serving. The more he serves and works in the church business office, the more he will enjoy the Lord's presence. Likewise, the more he records the information of the saints, cleans, and carries out other chores, the more he will touch the Lord and receive the supply of life. In this way, he knows that his serving is right.

Sometimes when a brother speaks in a meeting of the church, the more he speaks, the more supply people receive, and the more he himself is inwardly satisfied. This proves that his speaking is not merely an outward arrangement in the way of organization but that it is the result of growth in the inner life. Such speaking will have impact upon the listeners. A brother may preach the gospel and speak of how the Lord Jesus died on the cross to bear man's sins; nevertheless, no one may be touched. Another brother may also preach concerning the Lord Jesus' death on the cross to bear man's sins; however, his speaking may touch those who are listening. Although he may speak only a few sentences, the listeners will immediately sense that they are sinners. As a result, they will repent and receive the Lord Jesus. If we want our speaking to touch and convict people, we must have the experience of repentance and confession. If we experience repentance and confession, we will speak from experience when we give a message concerning the Lord Jesus bearing our sins. This will touch and convict people, causing them to touch life inwardly.

The best test of whether or not our service is according to life is our inner sense. Wherever we serve and whatever our service is, the best test is our inner sense. The more we serve, the more we should touch life, and the more we should experience the anointing; however, if the more we serve, the drier we become, we should stop our service and come back to the Lord to deal with our situation carefully. If those whom we visit do not reap the issue of life, and if those who listen to our speaking do not receive the supply of life, whether we are elders, deacons, or teachers, we should be clear inwardly that our position is wrong. In other words, our service is purely organizational. It is not the outgrowth of life. If this is the case, we need to seriously repent before the Lord in order to see where we have gone wrong in regard to life.

SAMUEL'S ANOINTING OF DAVID BEING THE BEST EXAMPLE OF A PROPER APPOINTING OF ELDERS

When the responsible brothers are arranging the services in the church, such as assigning a brother to be responsible in a district, a sister to be a deaconess, or a saint to be responsible for a specific service, they must be serious before the Lord and say to Him, "Lord, the authority is in Your hand. We do not have our own opinion. We want to touch Your feeling and act according to Your will." If they hold their own opinions and decisions and do not touch the Lord's feeling in making arrangements, this means that the Lord does not have authority over them. In other words, they may think that a certain one should take care of a particular service; however, when they are quietly in the presence of the Lord, they may have a feeling that the Lord disagrees with and rejects their consideration. Even though they approve, the Lord within disapproves. At this time, they should yield the authority to the Lord. On the surface, it is a group of responsible brothers who make the arrangement, but actually, it is the Lord who holds the authority.

When the co-workers appoint elders, they must be able to say from a pure conscience and a calm spirit, "We sense that this is the Lord's feeling. This is not our concept, our opinion, or our preference. It is not because we love these ones that we want them to be elders. Rather, we have considered and prayed before the Lord, and we have sought, waited, and looked to the Lord. We have sought to touch the Lord's feeling regarding every brother." This is what happened when Samuel anointed David. The decision did not depend upon what Samuel thought of David; rather, Samuel listened to Jehovah's speaking. It was not Samuel who held the authority in his hand but Jehovah. Samuel was simply a prophet of Jehovah. He was a man sent by Jehovah to be Jehovah's messenger. The authority was not in Samuel's hand. This is the basic principle in regard to co-workers' appointing of elders.

Samuel's anointing of David is the best example (1 Sam. 16:1-13). In this kind of appointing, God is allowed to speak; that is, He is allowed to have the authority. God never turned over this authority to any apostle. We should never think that if we are an apostle, we have the authority in ourselves to appoint elders. It is wrong to think this way. God never gives such authority to man. He always keeps authority in His hand. We have to fear God to the extent that we see that we are simply slaves. Authority is not in our hand. We are not the Lord. He is the Lord. In the church of God no brother or sister or group of saints should be so presumptuous as to usurp the Lord's authority. We need to have a God-fearing heart. Whenever we assign someone to serve, inwardly we need to bow down and worship, saying, "Lord, You are the Head of the church, and You are our Lord. Although You have entrusted us with the responsibility of making this assignment, the authority is in Your hand. Lord, we make this decision in Your name. What we say does not count. Only what You say counts. Lord, our discernment is not accurate. Yours is accurate." This is what it means to bear authority.

TWO KINDS OF SUBMISSION TO AUTHORITY

All the brothers and sisters who are arranged to serve should not consider that since it is the arrangement of the elders, they should simply obey. This is to submit to the authority of man, not of God. We should all realize that in the church God has the authority, Christ is the Head, and the elders are but God's deputy authority. We obey the elders because we submit to the authority of the Head. We are not submitting to the authority of man but to Christ, the Head of the church, recognizing His authority in the church.

There are two kinds of submission to authority. When some people submit to authority, a person can sense that they are submissive, but when others submit, their submission has the flavor of Christ the Head. For example, some people are humble; however, a person can sense only that they are humble and that there is no flavor of Christ in their humility. In contrast, the humility of others has the flavor of Christ. If we submit to someone merely because he is an elderly brother or because he is an elder, this will give people only the taste of submission, not the taste of Christ. However, when we submit to the elderly brothers and the elders based on God having the authority and Christ being the Head of the church, our submission to them is the result of our submission to the authority of the Head. The flavor is very different.

We can solemnly testify that the submission of some brothers and sisters causes us to fear God, because in their submission we touch Christ the Head. When these saints submit to the brothers, they cause the brothers to fear God, because the brothers touch the authority of the Head in their submission. Some may say, "If this is the case, should not these brothers be occupying a higher position?" We must be clear that this thought is not proper. This thought is despicable and offensive to God. Whether one is a deputy authority or one who submits to a deputy authority, if a person truly knows the authority of the Head, he will enable others to touch Christ the Head in him. The young brothers and sisters may be too young in the Lord to be in a position of representing authority, but if they truly know the authority of the Head and submit to those who represent authority, they will cause others to sense Christ the Head in them. As a result, others will sense the authority of the Head. They will sense the authority of the Head not in those to whom the young people submit but in the young people themselves. This will cause those who observe the young people to have a heart that fears the Lord.

The Lord can testify for me that a number of times I have observed this kind of situation. As a result, I truly have the fear of the Lord within me because I have touched His authority in the submission of the young ones. We should never consider this matter as the submission of subordinates to superiors such as occurs in human society. Although that kind of submission has its value and we appreciate it, submission as related to the organization of the Body far surpasses the submission found in human society. This is a solemn matter. It is most offensive to the Lord for a person in the church to make arrangements concerning a certain matter or person without inwardly touching the authority of the Head.

We should never have an opinion or make an arrangement outside the authority of the Head. To do so is offensive to the Lord.

BEING ACCORDING TO ORDER

The organization of the church is according to life, the authority of God, function, and ministry. In addition, the organization of the church is according to order. Order is related to authority; nevertheless, there is a distinction between the two.

We have seen that the organization of the church is not two-dimensional but three-dimensional. As types of the church, both a building and a human body are three-dimensional. The more "three-dimensional" a church is, the stronger it is. A weak church is a flat church. The flatter it is, the weaker it is. When a church is flat, it has no usefulness. If there are one hundred brothers and sisters in a church and nearly all are the same, this church is flat. A flat object, such as a flat metal sheet, often does not have much usefulness. However, if a bucket, a three-dimensional object, was formed from the metal sheet, it would become very useful.

In order for a church with one hundred brothers and sisters to function properly, there is a need for a clear order among the saints. One should be here and another there. When all are in the proper order, that church becomes functional as a three-dimensional entity. To be three-dimensional is to have an order, as spoken of in 1 Corinthians 12:28: "First apostles, second prophets, third teachers." This is an order. A proper family or couple can never be "flat." If the husband and wife occupy the same position, they cannot represent a proper human relationship, much less be a proper type of Christ and the church. Likewise, if children and parents are on the same level, occupying the same position, this would be an ugly condition.

The condition of some churches is flat. The flat condition is due to an arrangement according to organization, not according to Spirit and life. We can discern whether or not the organization of a church is according to Spirit and life by seeing whether the church is three-dimensional and has a proper order. Whether thirty people or three hundred people are gathered together, there should be order. Moreover, in every service in the church, there should be an order. There needs to be an order among those who sweep the floors and wipe the tables and among those who cook and set the tables for the love feasts. When every service is three-dimensional, this is a beautiful scene.

The church of God is like a body in which every bone must be joined to another. Every member must be coordinated with another member. Consequently, some members occupy a higher position, and others occupy a lower position. This is unavoidable. It is most foolish if some in the church would contend and ask why they occupy a lower position than others. In a human body, would it not be foolish for the feet to insist on occupying the same position as the eyes? Likewise, in the Body it is foolish to compete or contend for a higher position. In this matter, we all need the Lord's grace.

In a proper church a person can touch life and authority, and he can see function and ministry. Moreover, he can see that the church is "three-dimensional" and has order. This order comes from the previous four items: life, authority, function, and ministry. Order is not the result of someone saying that one person is above a second and under a third. This kind of order is useless. If Paul had spoken in this way, it would have indicated that he was a person who knew neither God's life nor God's authority and had neglected function and ministry.

If a co-worker knows life, authority, function, and ministry and if based upon these matters he tells a church that a certain brother is an elder, all those who fear and love the Lord will bow their heads and say Amen. This is not man's arrangement but something according to life, authority, function, and ministry. The more those in the church experience life, submit to the authority of the Lord, manifest their functions, and some among them carry out their particular ministry, the more there will be order and the less there will be chaos in the church.

When a church is facing a problem, we should not speak too much but should simply say, "O Lord, let the elders be clear concerning this matter." This means that we have to keep the order and recognize that the problem is the responsibility of the elders, not our responsibility. If someone sees that all the brothers and sisters are in order in the church, he will bow his head and worship, saying, "Indeed, God is among you." Likewise, when we see a church in which everyone is in order, we also will surely bow our head and worship the Lord for His presence among the saints. I hope that we would not receive these matters as doctrines or merely apply them to others; rather, we should apply them to ourselves and soberly put them into practice.

ALL PROBLEMS BEING THE RESULT OF NOT KEEPING THE ORDER

In 1948 after the victory in the Sino-Japanese War many of our brothers and sisters moved to Shanghai. Due to the Lord's sovereign arrangement, many senior brother co-workers were not in Shanghai at that time. As a result, the decisions regarding many important matters fell upon me. Among us there were several sister co-workers who had learned much and who kept their proper place in the order. They kept the proper order to such an extent that I desired to be a sister. It is wonderful to be a sister because a sister can check with the brothers concerning every matter. We should not think that it is comfortable to be in a higher position. The most comfortable thing is for a person to stand in the position that the Lord has given him. If he remains in his position, he will be satisfied and at ease. We should not think that it is more satisfying to direct people to do things. Being satisfied and at ease is not a matter of directing people or being directed. It altogether depends upon whether or not we keep the proper order.

Some people may ask, "How do we know if we are in the proper order?" One who asks such a question demonstrates that he is not in the proper order. Every believer knows whether or not he is in the proper order. Many brothers are not at rest in regard to their position. They are not inwardly satisfied and have no rest. In contrast, in my family I have several children, and they all know who is the oldest, the second oldest, and the third. Because they all know their respective positions, they are inwardly satisfied, pleased, and at rest. Many people have no rest in their service because their heart is not satisfied. They are not content with the place assigned to them by God. Consequently, they are neither pleased nor at rest.

If the organization of a church is according to life, the authority of God, function, and ministry, and has a three-dimensional order, the church will be strong and functioning.

A SUMMARY

The coordination and organization within the church must be according to life, the authority of God, function, ministry, and order. Only when all five requirements are met will the organization of the church be organic. We do not deny that the church has organization, but we must determine that the organization of the church is according to these five matters. All the arrangement and coordination in the church must be according to life, authority, function, ministry, and order. We must be strict in regard to these requirements.

We should not speak these words only to others; we need to speak them to ourselves. Every one of us must consider his own situation. Instead of taking these words as doctrines, each of us should use them to realistically examine our personal situation. Our present concern is that the church will become a dead organization. Rather than correcting this matter with our human hand, may we look to the Holy Spirit to work within us.

The Roman Catholic Church and the degraded Protestant churches have fallen into their present condition because they have problems in regard to these five matters. On our part we must always ask the Lord, "Am I in my proper place in the church with respect to my portion?"

CHAPTER FIVE

THE PRACTICE OF THE ORGANIZATION OF THE CHURCH

(1)

The previous chapters cover five points related to the organization of the church. Having seen these five basic points clearly, we now come to the practice related to the organization of the church. Although it may seem that we are studying merely external matters, these matters are very much related to our service and life. Some people think that it is sufficient to be spiritual and that there is no need to study in-depth the outward matters such as the organization of the church. This may sound reasonable, but the attitude is wrong. Those who neglect the organization of the church will surely suffer loss in their service and spiritual life.

Even though the Bible does not contain a charter for the organization of the church, it does contain the fact of the organization of the church. Human beings are not born with a list of rules and regulations; nevertheless, because we are living persons, we naturally have certain laws and principles operating within us. Only man-made organizations require rules and regulations. Since the church is a living entity, the Bible does not contain outward rules related to its organization. Although there are no organizational regulations concerning the church, we should study it in the same way that medical people study a human body.

Although we cannot set up rules for the composition of the body, in order to maintain its health we should know the function of each part of the body and its relationship to the other members. Not only doctors but everyone should know the structure of the human body. In the same way, every healthy

Christian, not only those serving the Lord, needs to know the organization of the church.

THE CONSTITUENTS OF THE CHURCH BEING GOD MINGLED WITH MAN AND MAN MINGLED WITH GOD

The human body as an organization has its basic constituents, and the church as an organization also has its basic constituents. The basic constituents of the church are people who have the life of God, that is, who are God mingled with man and man mingled with God. On the one hand, from a superficial view the constituents of the church are those who have God's life. These are not nominal Christians, because nominal Christians are the constituents of Christendom, not the church. The deeper view is that the constituents of the church are God plus man and man plus God. If there is only man, there is no church, and if there is only God, there is also no church. The church is the mingling of both God and man. The church is constituted of God and of man; both are necessary.

The church is composed of two elements: God and man. Only when both elements are present and are mingled together can there be the church. When we speak of the constituents of the church, we should not speak merely of the saved ones. This is not adequate. We must have a deeper view; that is, the church is the mingling of man with God.

As a constituent of the church God is not merely God the Creator but more precisely God mingled with man. As a basic constituent of the church, He is God incarnated, crucified, and resurrected. After having passed through incarnation, crucifixion, and resurrection, God has two elements: divinity and humanity. Many people, when they are newly saved, believe that the Savior whom they have received is simply God. Before incarnation, God was simply God, but after the incarnation, death, and resurrection of Christ, God is in man, and man is in God. If we touch this matter in a deep and detailed way, we will see that God went through a process that involved incarnation, death, resurrection, and ascension. In brief, we need to realize that as a basic constituent of the church, God is not simply God but God mingled with man.

If we desire to know the organization of the church, we must realize that God and man are its basic constituents. Man is a constituent of the church. As a constituent, man cannot be removed from the church. Without man there is no church. However, if there is only man and not God, there would also be no church. If humanity was removed and only the Spirit remained, this Spirit would not be the Spirit of the God who became flesh. In order to know God, a person must know the church, and in order to know man, a proper man, he must also know the church. The church is the mingling of God and man. Man cannot be missing from any item or aspect related to the church. The church is a mingling of divinity and humanity. If we know this, many problems in the church will spontaneously disappear. We do not desire to study the mere outward appearance of the church but to discover the basic principles concerning the church.

The Bible reveals that even the appointment of elders in the church is a matter of the mingling of God with man and of man with God. On the one hand, God works in a group of brothers and causes them to grow in life; on the other hand, God appoints them to be elders through the coordination of the apostles with the Holy Spirit (Acts 14:23; 20:28). When the apostles appoint elders, they surely need to seek the leading of the Holy Spirit through prayer, but they also need to use their discernment and judgment. When it is necessary to appoint elders, the apostles need to tell the Lord, "O Lord, You do not appoint the elders directly, but You entrust this matter to men. Nonetheless, may You be the One who makes the decision."

This is a solemn matter. Throughout the generations many activities in the church have been carried out either in one extreme or in the other. Some believers are too spiritual, and others are too rational. Any activity carried out according to either extreme is wrong. God must administrate the church through man. In the administration of the church, man must submit to the authority of God and let Him rule. If we touch the feeling of the Holy Spirit, we will see that every matter in the church is accomplished by God mingling Himself with man. The principle of the New Jerusalem is the same. In the New Jerusalem God dwells with man.

THE UNIVERSAL AND LOCAL ASPECTS OF THE CHURCH

The Definition of These Two Aspects

Two aspects of the church are that it is universal and local. The basic constituent of the church is a matter of the mingling of God and man, but the existence and expression of the church are related to its universal and local aspects. In itself the church is not local but universal. In the universe there is only one church, just as there is only one Christ. In the universe there is only one Head, Christ, and there is only one Body, the church.

We should never think of the church as being something local. In itself the church is not local but altogether universal. Although the church is universal, the expression of the church in this age is local. It is expressed in locality after locality. This is similar to the moon. Even though there is only one moon, it appears where we are, and it also appears in other places. There is only one moon, but it appears in numerous places. Hence, in regard to the organization of the church, we must see that the church has a universal aspect as well as a local aspect.

Universally the church is the church, whereas locally a church is a local expression of the universal church. The local expression of the church is the representation of the church in a locality. The local expression of the church is the representation of the church in a particular locality at a particular time. In other words, the church is fully represented by its expression in a particular locality. Hence, the Bible speaks of the church as being uniquely one (Eph. 1:22b-23), yet it also speaks of numerous churches. For example, it speaks of seven churches in Asia (Rev. 1:4). *Church* refers to the church's universal aspect, whereas *churches* refers to the local aspect. With respect to the church being universal, there is only one church; with respect to its local expression, there are tens of thousands of churches. If we do not have a clear understanding of the universal and local aspects of the church, we will encounter many problems.

The Error of the Roman Catholic Church

The Roman Catholic Church has wrongly applied the terms *catholic* and *universal*. It applies the universal aspect of the church to the local expression of the church. This is wrong. The word *catholic* can be rendered "universal" or "unified." However, the local expression of the church cannot be universalized or unified. Instead, the church is expressed in locality after locality. For example, in the New Testament the church was expressed as the church in Jerusalem, the church in Antioch, and the church in Ephesus. Today it is expressed in other cities, such as the church in Taipei and the church in London. All these local expressions of the church should not be unified. Once there is unification, an organization that is wrong will be produced. The Roman Catholic Church attempts to unify the local expressions of the church. This is erroneous.

The Roman Catholic Church is not entirely heretical. It contains a certain amount of truth; however, it mixes the truth, the fine flour, with leaven (Matt. 13:33; Rev. 2:18-29). Fine flour signifies the truth, whereas leaven signifies heresies. The Roman Catholic Church does have a basis for its application of the universal aspect of the truth. Its mistake, however, is that it extends the application of the universal nature of the church to the church's local expressions. The universality of the church should not be organizationally applied to the local expressions of the church. The universality of the church refers to the church itself, not to its expressions. If the universality of the church is applied to its local expressions, the church will become a catholic, or unified, church, that is, the Roman Catholic Church. The result of such unification is the papal city of the Roman Catholic Church, today's Vatican, the Holy See. Today tens of thousands of Catholic groups and organizations exist in different localities throughout the world. They have been unified and made subject to the rule of the Vatican. This is a huge error and is absolutely not according to the universal aspect of the church. The result of such unification is that the church loses her local expression, her direct fellowship with the Head, and the freedom of the Spirit to be expressed locally.

The Church Not Having a Headquarters

In view of the two aspects of the church, we cannot but say that the church is one. Since it is one, should the church in

Tainan and the church in Taipei be separated? If they are separated, how could they be one? Should the church in Tainan then control the church in Taipei, or should the church in Taipei control the church in Tainan? This question is the reason that the Roman Catholic Church came into existence. The unification of the churches produced an organization that included many churches of different ranks and levels. Churches on a lower level were under the control of churches on a higher level. As a result of the development of this system of hierarchy, the Vatican came into existence. The error of the Roman Catholic Church lies in its neglect of the independence of the local churches in regard to the church's local expression. This is to say that the Roman Catholic Church confuses the universal nature of the church with its local expression. This is truly a serious problem.

When we come to the matter of the organization of the church, we must know the basic constituents of the church. Then we need to know the two basic aspects of the church. On one hand, the church is uniquely one, but on the other hand, in regard to its expression, there are tens of thousands of churches. In other words, the church is universal, but its expression is local. In the Bible God did not place one local church above another local church; neither did God choose one church to be the center and headquarters of the local churches. The church in Jerusalem was not the headquarters, nor did the church in Antioch become the headquarters of the churches among the Gentiles.

In the Bible there is no evidence of a superior church, or of a headquarters. Even in the most degraded stage of the church, that is, in Revelation when the Lord wrote the seven epistles to the seven local churches, He still addressed all the churches on the same level. Some Christians have portrayed the seven churches in Asia as seven lamps on a single lampstand. According to their understanding, the lampstand is the headquarters, and the seven lamps are seven sub-churches. Not only is such a portrayal inaccurate, the implication is also wrong. The seven epistles in Revelation present seven golden lampstands. This indicates that the Lord considers each church to be on the same level. Moreover, each church was accountable to the Lord directly, and not one was accountable to another. Every church has the same standing before the Lord, and no church is above another. The church in Ephesus was not accountable to the church in Smyrna, and the church in Smyrna did not control the church in Pergamos. Moreover, the church in Pergamos was not above the church in Thyatira. No church controlled another.

I am concerned that many of the newly saved brothers and sisters may hold a wrong concept, considering the church in Taipei to be the headquarters among us. The church in Taipei is a large local church, but it is not the headquarters. In the Bible there is no concept of the church having a headquarters. We cannot use the universal aspect of the church as a basis for the unification of the local churches. This is erroneous. In regard to the church itself, it is one; but in regard to its local expression, there are tens of thousands of churches. We must uphold both aspects of the church; otherwise, we will encounter problems.

Not only have the Roman Catholic Church and the Greek Orthodox Church committed this great error, but the Protestant churches have also been deeply influenced by the practice of having a headquarters with each group having its respective headquarters. This practice causes the churches to lose their local expression. It is acceptable for a large local church to assist a smaller local church, but it is wrong for the larger local church to assume a higher position than that of the smaller local church and to take control of it.

THE ORGANIZATION OF THE CHURCH
HAVING TWO ASPECTS

The church has both a universal and a local aspect, and its organization also has a universal and a local aspect.

In terms of organization, the apostles are related to the universal church. In the Scriptures none of the apostles were apostles in relation only to a single local church. The office of an apostle is universal, not local, whereas the office of an elder or a deacon is local. If an elder in the church in Kaohsiung moves to Taipei, he will not necessarily be appointed an elder of the church in Taipei. If a person has been appointed to be an elder in one locality, he does not automatically continue in that office should he move somewhere else. If a brother is an elder in Kaohsiung, he may not even be appointed to be a deacon if he moves to Taipei. However, an apostle will continue to be an apostle whether he is in Kaohsiung or Taipei. Offices related to a locality are restricted to that locality. However, apostleship is not restricted to a particular locality.

The basic constituents of both the universal church and the local churches are the same; that is, in both its universal and local aspects the church is constituted of people who have the life of Christ. However, there is a distinction in regard to the offices in the church. This distinction corresponds to the churches universal and local aspects. The office of an apostle is altogether related to the universal church, whereas the office of an elder or deacon is related only to a local church. The sphere of these offices should never be confused.

THE DISTINCTION BETWEEN OFFICES AND GIFTS

The Definition of Offices and Gifts

According to the organization of the church, there is a distinction between the offices related to the universal and local aspects of the church. Moreover, there is also a distinction between office and gift. Being an elder or a deacon is a matter of office, not gift. However, to speak for God as a prophet is a matter of gift, not office. All offices are on the administrative side, and all gifts are on the spiritual side. In other words, offices are for administration and government, and gifts are for spiritual building up. These two aspects are closely related, yet they are quite distinct from each other.

According to the universal and local aspects of the church, the office of the apostles and the offices of the elders and deacons are not related to the same sphere. Apostles are universal, whereas elders and deacons are local. To be an apostle, elder, or deacon is a matter of office. However, to be a prophet, teacher, or evangelist is not a matter of office. Among the offices in the church, in the universal aspect as well as the local aspect, apostles have the highest office, then elders, and then deacons. Each has an office in the church.

Among the gifts there is also a distinction. Some gifts are for the church, and some are for individuals. The gifts that God gives to the church are for the church, and the gifts that He gives to an individual are related to the individual. The gifts given by God to the church are persons, as spoken of in Ephesians 4:7-16. After Christ ascended to heaven, He gave various gifts to the church. He gave some as apostles and some as prophets and some as evangelists and some as shepherds and teachers (v. 11). Christ gave these persons as gifts to the church. The church receives these gifts; thus, they are for the church.

The gifts that individuals receive are spiritual abilities and capabilities. Through the Holy Spirit, God gives certain individuals the ability to teach. This ability is a gift given to them by God. Such gifts are referred to as gifts for individuals. Among these gifts for individuals, some are ordinary and others are miraculous. Ordinary gifts are those spoken of in Romans 12:4-21. Love for one another is included among these gifts. Our seeing the brothers off at the train station is also a matter of an ordinary gift. According to Romans 12, the gifts that we have received are different. Some of us do one thing, and others do something else. Some may love people, and others may give hospitality. These gifts are ordinary gifts given to individuals.

The other kind of gifts are the miraculous gifts spoken of in 1 Corinthians 12:9-10. These include speaking in tongues, interpreting tongues, healing, and carrying out operations of works of power. However, there is a gift that is both ordinary and miraculous. This is the gift of prophecy. To prophesy is to speak for God and speak forth God, including predicting and foretelling. The emphasis in 1 Corinthians 12 is predicting, which is miraculous, whereas in Romans 12 the emphasis is not on predicting but on speaking for God as a prophet. The Greek word translated "prophesy" also means "predict." Every person who functions as a mouthpiece of God speaks for God and thus is a prophet. Sometimes a person's speaking may be a prediction, and sometimes it may be an ordinary teaching.

The ordinary teaching rendered by a prophet is related to his regular spiritual learning. Based on his regular learning, when he is inspired, he will rise up to speak for the edification of the saints. This is to prophesy. Strictly speaking, this is not predicting. It is an ordinary gift. At another time a person may have the instant inspiration of the Holy Spirit and rise up to speak a word of prediction. This is what happened in the case of Agabus. He rose up and predicted that there was about to be a great famine over the whole inhabited earth (Acts 11:27-28). His prediction was a miraculous gift, as spoken of in 1 Corinthians 12, and was the result of inspiration.

According to the organization of the church, there is a distinction between the offices as they relate to the universal and local aspects of the church, and there is also a distinction between offices and gifts. With respect to offices, they either are related to the universal church or to the local church. With respect to gifts, they are either for the church or for individuals. In the entire Bible only three portions speak of gifts. The first portion is Ephesians 4, which tells us that some gifts were given by Christ to the church. The second portion is Romans 12, which speaks of ordinary gifts, such as showing mercy. The third portion is 1 Corinthians 12, which speaks of miraculous gifts, such as speaking in tongues, interpretation of tongues, and healing. The following outline shows the distinctions between the types of offices and the types of gifts:

I. Offices:
   A. Universal—apostles.
   B. Local—elders and deacons.
II. Gifts:
   A. For the church (Eph. 4).
   B. For individuals:
      1. Ordinary gifts (Rom. 12).
      2. Miraculous gifts (1 Cor. 12).

Strictly speaking, the apostleship is the only office in the universal church, but in a broader sense prophets as well as shepherds and teachers are also offices in the universal church.

How do we distinguish between offices and gifts? To have an office is a matter of appointment, whereas to have a gift is a matter of ability. For example, to be a carpenter is a matter of ability, but to become a foreman is a matter of office. Although two carpenters may have the same ability, one may be a senior foreman and the other a junior foreman. Even though both have the same ability, they may have different offices. Let us use another example. On one hand, to be a teacher is a matter of gift; on the other hand, it is an office. In terms of the ability to teach, a teacher has a gift, but in terms of being hired to teach, a teacher has an office. This should be very clear.

The Importance of Offices and Gifts

In the church both the gifts and the offices are indispensable. An office may be compared to a husband, and a gift, to a wife; we should never emphasize one and neglect the other. Nevertheless, in their spiritual pursuit, most Christians pay more attention to gifts than to offices.

Throughout the centuries there have always been problems in regard to the organization of the church. Most of the problems have been due to offices. Gifts tend to be less problematic, but it is very easy for problems and mistakes to arise in relation to offices. If a person is not gifted yet claims to be gifted, others quickly can detect his lack of gift. However, it may be difficult to tell whether or not a person has a certain office. While it is difficult to pretend to have a gift, it is much easier to pretend to have an office. This is why the matter of having an office gives rise to more problems than the matter of having a gift. There is no human hand in the formation of gifts. People cannot arrange for someone to be a prophet or for another to be an evangelist. However, human hands are involved in the appointment of offices. The appointment of offices must pass through human hands, as in the laying on of hands by the apostles in Acts 14:23 and Titus 1:5. Church history tells us that the majority of the problems in the church are due to offices. This is why most of those who pursue the Lord desire gifts and despise offices. However, it is not sufficient to have only gifts.

Office is a matter of authority, and gift is a matter of spirituality. First Corinthians 12 is a chapter on spiritual gifts. When the church lacks gifts, it lacks spiritual things. However, gifts are not life. There is a difference between the two. The primary requirement for someone to speak as a prophet is that he must be spiritual; that is, he must have the Holy Spirit operating in him. In recent years many people have paid too much attention to spirituality and disregarded authority. This is to be extreme. On the other hand, in organized Christianity the emphasis is altogether related to office, to man's authority, and gifts are neglected. This is also to be extreme. Although some preachers have been appointed to their offices, they do not have the gift of preaching. Their appointment is merely an official arrangement, and it is a mistake. Hence, although they are appointed to be "carpenters," they do not know how to use a "hammer." However, if we try to correct such mistakes by caring only for gifts and neglecting offices, this will also be a mistake. In the organization of the church there must be gifts as well as offices. In the church there needs to be spirituality as well as authority.

If in the church there are only gifts, there will be no authority, and if there are no gifts, there will be no offices. If there are spiritual gifts in the church, there should also be authority; otherwise, the church will be weak. Under normal conditions a church should take care of both matters: spirituality and authority. When both these matters are properly coordinated, all the problems of the church will be solved spontaneously.

CHAPTER SIX

THE PRACTICE OF THE ORGANIZATION OF THE CHURCH

(2)

CONCERNING OFFICES

In the organization of the church there is a distinction between office and gift. An office is a matter of authority, whereas a gift is a matter of spirituality. God has determined that in the organization of the church there is authority as well as spirituality. The problems that the church has encountered throughout the centuries have been due to a lack of either spirituality or authority; that is, there have been problems in regard to either the gifts or the offices. Our intention in our current study is not to search for regulations in the Bible. Rather, we want to see God's purpose in regard to the organization of the church. In other words, we want to find out why God desires that there be organization in the church. As we touch the deeper meanings of this matter, we will see that it is ultimately related to authority and spirituality. If the organization of the church is according to God's desire, authority will be established and spirituality will be manifested in the church. In other words, the church will have both authority and spirituality.

Apostles

Not Being Appointed by Man

Authority does not come from man. Offices, therefore, do not depend on human hands. In the church the first office is that of apostles. Apostles are not appointed by man. The authority, office, and position of apostles do not come from man. Although human hands may be involved in the appointment of elders and deacons, absolutely no human hand is involved in the appointment of apostles because apostles are universal, whereas elders and deacons are local.

The offices of the apostles, elders, and deacons show that in the church there is authority and order. In this regard, not every office is on the same level. However, in regard to any office, we need to pay attention to one matter—the source of authority. Outwardly, apostles appoint elders and deacons. The authority of the elders is given to them by the apostles, although, strictly speaking, the apostles only confirm the authority of the elders and deacons. Hence, in a proper church life no one becomes an elder of his own accord; rather, elders are designated and appointed by the apostles. Only when an apostle designates certain ones to be elders do they have the position and authority of elders in the church. Nevertheless, the source of the elders' authority is Christ, the Head of the church, because it is He, not man, who has appointed the apostles. We should not despise the matter of appointment. Although Paul was spiritual, he still made many arrangements. In the organization of the church there are two kinds of appointments: appointments made by the Head directly and appointments carried out through human hands.

Since no human hand or human confirmation is involved in the appointment of apostles, there is a possibility for some people to make a false claim of apostleship. Thus, in the church there is the need to try the apostles. In Revelation the Lord commended the church in Ephesus, saying, "You have tried those who call themselves apostles and are not, and have found them to be false" (2:2). The elders and deacons are appointed by the apostles. If the elders and deacons were directly appointed by the Head, there would be many false elders and deacons, and authority within the church would be greatly confused. To avoid such confusion, God appoints apostles, and apostles appoint elders. God does not want His authority to be in a state of confusion in the church. God also does not want the church itself to be in confusion.

Being Sent by God

God Himself appoints apostles and sends them out (Rom.

1:1; 1 Cor. 12:28; 1 Tim. 2:7; 2 Tim. 1:11). Since there is no outward appointment or assignment by man, people may doubt a person's apostleship (1 Cor. 9:1-3). However, no one should doubt the eldership. When an apostle appoints certain ones to be elders, everyone is able to see it, and thus there should be no doubt about it. In contrast, people may question one's apostleship. Moreover, due to the absence of human participation in the appointment of apostles, there may be false apostles (2 Cor. 11:13; Rev. 2:2). However, no one can be a false elder or a false deacon, because elders and deacons are appointed by apostles. Such an appointment cannot be falsified.

Who are the apostles? This is an important question. For the past two thousand years, no one has dared to say who is an apostle. No one dares to say that he himself is an apostle; neither is anyone willing to say that others are apostles. In Christianity some people even hold an erroneous concept that there were only twelve apostles. In the Gospels there were twelve apostles, in Acts there were twelve apostles, and in the coming New Jerusalem there will also be twelve apostles. Because of this, some think that there are no apostles in addition to the twelve apostles. They do not believe that there is a thirteenth apostle. However, according to the Bible their reasoning is not sound. In Acts 14:14 Paul and Barnabas are spoken of as "the apostles." Thus, in the Scriptures there is at least a thirteenth apostle. This is strong proof that the term *apostle* is not limited only to the twelve but that there are many more.

The twelve apostles spoken of in the Gospels and Acts have a special place. Their names will be on the foundations of the wall of the New Jerusalem. Nevertheless, we must see that they are not the only apostles. Some in Christianity say that there are no more apostles because the so-called apostolic age is over. This is wrong. According to the principle of the Bible, we are still in the apostolic age. There have been numerous apostles throughout the past two thousand years.

What kind of person can be an apostle? To be an apostle involves the matter of authority. Authority is a great matter. When we speak concerning the organization of the church, we touch the matter of office and thus the matter of authority. It is marvelous that God never allows another to be the source of authority. He does not allow man to touch authority or let it be initiated by man's hand. Hence, no one can appoint another person to be an apostle. The authority to appoint an apostle has always been in the hands of the Head. Since men do not appoint apostles, the office of an apostle may be questioned. In contrast, since apostles appoint elders and deacons, the offices of elders or deacons need not be held in question.

God has given the apostles authority to appoint elders; hence, when there is an accusation against an elder, it may be presented to the apostles (1 Tim. 5:19). The apostles do have authority in regard to the elders. Some have said that there are no more apostles and that the apostolic age is over; however, if this were the case, there would be a great problem. If there were no apostles in the church, there would be no authority and order, and everything would be dependent on gifts. If the church had only gifts and there were no offices, the church would undoubtedly become flat and no longer be three-dimensional.

Who are apostles? Who has received authority directly from the Lord? This is a solemn matter. Although the Roman Catholic Church is three-dimensional in its hierarchy, its way is erroneous. It claims that the pope is Christ's representative, a successor of Peter. All the cardinals are subject to the pope. In turn, they have authority to rule over the bishops. Although the Roman Catholic Church is altogether three-dimensional, it is the pope who is the ultimate source of authority in the Catholic Church. What an erroneous hierarchy!

In the Bible no apostle is under another apostle. As an apostle, Timothy was led by Paul. However, Paul was not above Timothy nor did he rule over Timothy. In the Bible the apostleship is not three-dimensional. It does not say that God placed one apostle above another apostle; neither does it say that one apostle was under another apostle. All apostles are subject to Christ the Head, and only the Head is above the apostles. Hence, apostleship is not three-dimensional. Otherwise, there would be a chief apostle, such as the pope in the Roman Catholic Church, and all authority would be vested in him.

Peter was not under Paul, nor was Paul under Peter. If Peter were above Paul, there would have been a great problem; that is, the churches of the Jews would have had authority over the churches of the Gentiles. If Paul were above Peter, the churches of the Gentiles would have had authority over the churches of the Jews. However, this was not the actual situation. Peter was under the Head, and Paul also was under the Head. The authority over the churches of the Jews was Christ, and also the authority over the churches of the Gentiles was Christ. Although the Bible contains the term *super-apostles*, it is not used in a positive sense. Paul said, "I count myself to be inferior to the super-apostles in nothing" (2 Cor. 11:5), and he also said, "I am the least of the apostles" (1 Cor. 15:9). The basic thought is that God never considered the apostleship to be three-dimensional; that is, there were never different levels, from lower to higher, among the apostles. The result of having such levels would be a top apostle, who is under Christ the Head but over the other apostles. This is the arrangement in the Roman Catholic Church.

Is the church flat or three-dimensional? The church is three-dimensional because the authority of the Head is within it. This does not mean that one church is above a second and under a third. The church is not a religious organization. Each local church is directly under the Head. One local church cannot control another local church. Every local church is directly under the Head. This is similar to an apostle being directly under the Head. If a person is sent by the Lord to do the Lord's work, he should be neither proud nor humble. If a person is an apostle, he will sense the Lord's presence. The Lord's presence is an apostle's authority.

The Proof of Apostleship Being the Fruit of an Apostle's Labor

Since the authority of the apostles comes from the Head, the source of authority in the organization of the church is surely the Head. However, who can be considered an apostle? The Corinthians questioned the apostleship of Paul, and he responded by saying, "If to others I am not an apostle, yet surely I am to you; for you in the Lord are the seal of my apostleship" (9:2). Paul's word here sounds like that of a parent speaking to his children. Parents may not be parents to others, yet surely they are parents to their children. First Corinthians 9 provides the strongest and clearest example of what it means to be an apostle.

To use more familiar terminology, an apostle can be compared to a father who has begotten children. In Paul's case he might not have been an apostle to others, but surely he was an apostle to the Corinthians. He asked them, "Are you not my work in the Lord?" (v. 1). This means that if he were not an apostle, how could the Corinthians have become believers? If he were not their father, how could there be believers in Corinth? The believers in Corinth were the seal of Paul's apostleship, that is, of his being a father. Not everyone is a father. Although a man may be fifty or eighty years old, he may not be a father. Only those who have begotten children are fathers.

To others Paul may not have been an apostle, yet surely he was to the Corinthians. They were his work in the Lord. To those who examined him, Paul replied, "You are the seal of my apostleship in the Lord." His defense was truly wise. We need to firmly understand a basic matter; that is, the fruit of a person's labor in the Lord is a proof of his apostleship. If a person preaches the gospel to the natives of Taiwan, labors for the Lord among them, saves and raises up some to serve God, and establishes a church, undoubtedly he is an apostle to these ones. It is meaningless for someone merely to consider himself to be an apostle or to feel that he is an apostle. Only the actual fruit of his work is proof of his apostleship.

However, we also need to ask ourself: Did I do the work by myself or in the Lord? Did I do the work on my own or was I sent by the Lord? A person doing a work must be certain of two matters: He must know that he has been sent by the Lord and that he is doing the work in the Lord. While others may not know whether our work is in the Lord, we ourselves should know. If a person does a certain work by himself and obtains positive results, these results alone are not proof of his apostleship. A person's work must be done in the Lord, with the Lord, and through being mingled with the Lord. The result will be proof of his apostleship.

The term *apostle* means "sent one." Every believer is able to sense if a person has been sent by the Lord to do the work and whether or not he is doing the work by himself. There is a difference. If I send someone to do something, he has my authority, but if he does something by himself, he does not have my authority. If the government sent me to do something, the authority of the government would be behind me; however, if I were to do something by myself, I may not have the proper authority. Although there is not much difference outwardly, there is a big difference inwardly.

Being One Who Submits to God's Authority and Who Is Sent by God

A person who works for the Lord must submit to the authority of the Head; he must be governed and controlled entirely by the Head. Such a worker does not go out by himself but is charged by the Holy Spirit and sent by the Head. Since he is sent and appointed by the Head, authority is with him. It may be difficult for people to determine whether or not he is an apostle, but he himself should have the assurance when he goes out to work that he is under the authority of the Head, controlled by the Head, and sent by the Head. A worker is sent by the Head to do the work of the Head; thus, he does not know what it means to be political in order to please people. If the Head did not send him, he would not do the work.

I can testify before the Lord whom I serve that when I encounter problems, I go to Him. I do not beg Him; rather, I say, "Lord, this is Your business and not mine. This is not my work but what You desire me to do." Concerning what we do, we need to ask ourselves whether the work is ours or the Lord's, and whether it is we who want to do it or the Lord who wants us to do it. If it is our work, and if it is we who want to do it, we will not have apostolic authority. Apostolic authority lies with the Head. In Acts 13:2 the Holy Spirit said, "Set apart for Me now Barnabas and Saul for the work to which I have called them." Hence, it is the Lord who sends, and it is His work that they do. The sending and the work are the Lord's.

After the Sino-Japanese War, I went to Nanking because I was very clear that the Lord wanted me to go there. Prior to this, the brothers in Nanking also had much prayer, not only for my coming but also for the many problems among us at that time, including personal problems and problems related to the entire work. According to my desire, I had planned to work in northern China, but after much prayer and seeking over a long period of time, I was clear that the Lord wanted me to go to Nanking. The first time I spoke in Nanking, I said, "I have come here with a burden, and I want to impart this burden into you." Not long after that, a brother with whom I was well acquainted came to visit me with the president of a certain seminary. According to courtesy and custom, I should have paid the president of the seminary a return visit. But when I went back to my room, the Lord spoke to me within: "I sent you here to work and not to please men. His coming to visit you is his business. He is also My child, My servant, and is responsible to Me. Who desires that you pay him a return visit?" The seminary president came to visit me, yet I did not pay him a return visit. It was not because of my pride but because of a strong forbidding within me. Since the Lord did not want me to go, I could not go. Moreover, I could not say anything, because I am not a diplomat or a politician. I was in the Lord's hand. I could only do what He wanted me to do.

Although I was in that city for an entire year, I did not visit any of the preachers. In this regard, I became a cold and impolite person. The Lord can testify that this was not due to my pride but due to the inner forbidding. The work in Nanking was not my work. To visit the preachers would have been of great convenience to the work, but I did not have the right to do so. Likewise, when I came to Taiwan, the situation was also very difficult. Many people asked me to visit certain ones, but the Lord spoke the same word to me again: "I brought you here to do My work and not to please men." The most important matter is whether the authority of the Head is with us. When we work for the Lord, are we concerned about behaving ourselves properly, or are we concerned about laboring as those sent by the Lord? If we desire to simply behave ourselves properly, we ourselves will have to take care of every aspect. Nevertheless, the authority of the Head will not be with us, and we will not be as those who are sent by Him for His work. If someone thinks that in the service his purpose is to help a certain brother, then it is better for him not to have a part in the service. No aspect of the work belongs to men. All the work belongs to the Head, the Lord of hosts. Some people say to me, "You have to bear so many burdens and take care of so many matters. How is it that you are always at rest and rejoicing?" I tell them, "Please consider: Is this my business? Is this my work? This is the Lord's business, the Lord's work. I do however much He wants me to do. He must take care of the rest." The workers need to be saved by reminding themselves constantly that the work which they do is the Lord's work, not their own work. If it is the Lord's work, the Lord has the authority and will bear the responsibility. If we do the work of the Lord of hosts, all those who serve Him on earth are our co-workers. If we do our own work, it is no wonder that we work alone.

An apostle is under the authority of the Head. To be an apostle is to be a sent one. If the Head has not sent us, it is meaningless for us to seek to be an apostle. No man can appoint us to be an apostle. Man does not have the authority to appoint apostles. Only when a person is under the Head, commissioned by the Head, and sent by the Head to do His work can he be an apostle. Even if others do not acknowledge him as an apostle, the Lord who sent him will still regard him as an apostle. Whoever the Head sends is an apostle, and the authority of the Head is with him.

No one can appoint others to be apostles. Whether or not a person is an apostle is not determined by others. The offices in the church are altogether a matter of the authority of the Head. If none of us submits to the authority of the Head, there will be no offices in the church. We might pray to receive the gift to give a few messages, but there will be no offices in the church. In order to have an office and represent authority in the church, we need to submit to the authority of the Head. There must be some who submit to the authority of the Head, who are sent by the Head, who fast and pray, and who wait for the Lord's command. There must be some who have heard, "Set apart for Me now Barnabas and Saul, not for their own work but for the work to which I have called them." Without authority, there will be no offices in the church, only gifts.

The desolate condition of Christianity is related to having gifts but not offices. When some are stirred up and zealous, they preach the gospel, give sermons, and obtain certain results; however, they do not have the authority of the Holy Spirit, the authority of the Head. They have only gifts but no offices. For the church to be strong and to meet the Lord's need in the present age, we must prostrate ourselves, submit to the authority of the Head, and say to Him, "Lord, I am here. What do You want to do?" The most important matter is not gifts but offices. Although some may not be able to give messages, when you contact them, you sense an authority that cannot be violated. This does not mean that they are presumptuous and have assumed a high position; on the contrary, they are surely men who prostrate themselves in dust and ashes.

Such a person would say to the Lord, "Lord, You are the Head, and I am a slave who has been bought by You. I prostrate myself. I do not have my work, my purpose, my future, my inclination, my choice, and my preference. Lord, I am a slave. I will say whatever You want me to say and do whatever You want me to do." The authority in such a one is definite. He is surely an apostle. He does not need to wear the label of an apostle. In him there is simply the authority of the Head. Once the church submits to the authority of the Head, immediately offices, authority, and order will be manifested. Then people will see that the church is strong and functioning.

CHAPTER SEVEN

THE PRACTICE OF
THE ORGANIZATION OF THE CHURCH

(3)

Proving an Apostle

The most difficult matter in regard to the organization of the church is the offices. For the past two thousand years, there have not been many problems in regard to the gifts. Because gifts are spiritual abilities, it is easy to tell whether or not someone has them. There is little ground for dispute. Consequently, most of the disputes are concerning offices. Offices are a matter of authority. To be an apostle, an elder, or a deacon is a matter of appointment, that is, a matter of authority. However, the appointment of apostles is very different from the appointment of elders and deacons. Whereas the appointment of apostles does not involve human hands, the appointment of elders and deacons passes through human hands and thus involves the element of man. In the Bible there is no record of people questioning the authority of elders and deacons, but there is a record of them questioning the authority of apostles.

There is no need to try, or prove, the office of the elders and deacons; however, there is a need to try the apostles (Rev. 2:2). It is not difficult to prove the office of the elders and deacons, but it is difficult to prove the office of apostles. Over the past two centuries some in the church have said that since there is no way to confirm the apostles, there is also no way to confirm the elders and deacons. If it were not possible to prove the office of the apostles, they felt that they had sufficient grounds to say that neither can the office of the elders and deacons appointed by apostles be confirmed. They felt that there should be no elders and deacons but only responsible brothers, since apostles are no longer with us and the apostolic age is over. Consequently, they called the elders "responsible brothers" and the deacons "serving brothers."

This indicates that the source of the problem lies with the office of the apostles. Since the appointment of apostles is entirely of God and does not pass through human hands, it is invisible and difficult for man to perceive. Even until today, we must confess that the confirmation of apostles is still a problem; however, if we were not so influenced by the background of degraded Christianity, this matter would not be difficult. I hope that we can empty ourselves of the influence of this background and return to the Bible to consider the matter of apostleship with a simple mind.

Apostles Having the Authority of God

First Corinthians 12:28 says, "God has placed some in the church: first apostles." We should not think of an apostle as being an extraordinary person, or that only people like Paul, Peter, and Timothy are worthy to be called apostles. Such a concept is inaccurate. Apostles are not extraordinary people. They are merely people whom God has sent and to whom He has given authority. Of course, a person cannot send another to do something for him unless he gives the person he is sending a certain amount of authority. Even if the sender sends him to do a very small thing, the sender must at least give him a small amount of authority.

If a person goes out to work for the Lord and his going is truly of the Lord, he will have the Lord's authority. However, if he is sent out by men, not by the Lord, and if his going out is of himself, he will not have the Lord's authority. Whether a worker is an apostle and has the Lord's authority are not matters which can be determined outwardly. Before the Lord, a worker must ask, "Am I sent by the Lord to do the work, or am I sent by men? Is my work based on the Lord's desire or on my own preference?" These questions must be answered before the Lord in a person's inner being.

Likewise, we must use our spirit to discern whether or not

another person is an apostle. Inwardly we must ask, "Does this one who serves the Lord come from the Lord or does he come of himself? Is he doing the work according to the Lord's desire or according to his own zeal?" We must use our spirit to answer these questions. If we acknowledge that a worker is from the Lord and that the Lord desires that he do the work, we must also acknowledge that he has authority. If we acknowledge that he is a worker sent by the Lord, that he is of the Lord, and that his work is according to the Lord's desire, we cannot deny that he has authority. It is not possible to determine a person's apostleship merely according to outward factors.

Paul said to the Corinthians, "If to others I am not an apostle, yet surely I am to you" (9:2). The principle in this verse is that Paul was an apostle to a certain group of believers, the Corinthians, but not necessarily to believers among whom he had not labored. If the Lord did not send him to work among a particular group, he would not have had the Lord's authority among them. For instance, although I am master of my house, I am not master of another person's house. In other words, although I may be an apostle in a certain place, when I go to another place, I may merely be a believer. I am not an apostle to a certain place, nor do I have authority in that place if the Lord has not sent me to work there.

I dare not assert that Paul was not an apostle to the churches in Judea, but I am sure that in the Gentile churches he had authority. He may not have had authority in the churches in Judea, because the Lord had not sent him to work among the Jews. However, the Gentile churches accepted Paul as an apostle because God had sent him to work among the Gentiles. Hence, for a person to determine whether or not he is an apostle, he must examine himself by asking, "Am I doing this work out of myself, or have I been sent by God?" Likewise, regarding whether a person is an apostle to us, we must ask ourselves, "Am I under the work that he has been sent by God to do?" If we are under this work, we must receive the authority of the one sent to carry out the work. We cannot accept only the work and not the authority. For example, when I am enrolled in a certain school, I have to accept the authority of the school.

In a sense, the matter of the apostleship is not too difficult. An apostle is not an extraordinary person in the church. There is only one great and extraordinary person in the church; He is our Lord Jesus. Besides Him, there is no other great or extraordinary person. All men are from the Lord. If there is a work that enables us to know the Lord, we have to humble ourselves and say, "The Lord's authority is here." We cannot accept a work yet reject the authority of the worker. There is not a single work that is without an authority. This is true not only in regard to the work of the Lord but also in regard to the work of men. If I were to ask a cook to buy some food, I would have to give him some authority. Without authority, he would not be able to do the work.

Those Who Are under the Work of an Apostle Needing to Submit to His Authority

The basic principle is that the Lord is the unique source of everything. An apostle is one who is sent by the Lord to do a work. Since he is sent by the Lord to do a work, he surely has received authority from the Lord. This authority is the apostolic authority. Hence, if we are under a person's work, accept his work, and receive benefit from his work, we must submit to the authority that he has been given to carry out the work. To submit to and accept the authority of a work is equivalent to recognizing the one entrusted with the work as an apostle.

If we think that an apostle has to be someone extraordinary, it will be very difficult to recognize anyone as an apostle. We must be delivered from this wrong concept and simply see that an apostle is one who is sent by the Lord to work for Him. Since the Lord has sent him to work, he must have received authority from the Lord. If this is our view, it will be easy for us to understand the matter of apostleship. The one from whom we receive the work of God is the one who has authority. To acknowledge his authority is to acknowledge that he is an apostle.

The problem today is that people will receive a work but not the authority of the one carrying out the work. This is neither according to the teaching of the Bible nor according to the order arranged by God. The Bible is full of order, and God always does things in an orderly way. We cannot receive our parents and reject their authority, nor can we receive our teachers and reject their authority. It is impossible to do so. An apostle may say that to a certain group of people he is not an authority, not an apostle, yet surely he is an apostle to certain ones because they were the result of his work. This corresponds to the example of the apostle Paul. To the church in Jerusalem or even to the church in Antioch, Paul may not have been considered an apostle, yet surely he was an apostle to the church in Corinth. If Paul were not an apostle, how did the Corinthians become believers?

For a church to be three-dimensional and strong, the saints must receive the authority of the apostle in the same way that they receive his work. Receiving an apostle's work yet denying God's authority in him is abnormal. Such a church will have absolutely no way to be strengthened or built up. It will surely be flat, not three-dimensional. For a church to be three-dimensional and strong, all the saints must receive the authority of the apostle in the same way they receive his work. In this way, they will become an apostle's living letter of commendation.

In 2 Corinthians 3:2-3 Paul said, "You are our letter, inscribed in our hearts, known and read by all men, since you are being manifested that you are a letter of Christ ministered by us, inscribed not with ink but with the Spirit of the living God; not in tablets of stone but in tablets of hearts of flesh." This means that the Corinthians were Paul's living letter of commendation. In one sense, it was the Holy Spirit who wrote through Paul, yet in another sense, it was Paul who wrote through the Holy Spirit. The content of Paul's letter was Christ. Paul inscribed Christ in the hearts of the Corinthians; hence, they became Paul's living letter of commendation. If a person has written such a living letter of commendation, he must be an apostle.

From this we see that the question concerning apostleship must be resolved not from without but from within. It is much easier to prove this matter inwardly. Although someone is not an apostle who has been commanded by God to do a work or been sent by God, he may claim and pretend to be an apostle. For instance, someone may go to labor in a certain city, but God may not have measured out to him a portion in the work there. God did not send him there or entrust him with the work in that city, yet he may claim to be an apostle to that city. For this reason we need to learn to discern the source of authority in the church. Even though a mother may be young, to the children born of her she is still a mother. This is a big test to those serving the Lord.

If we say that we are apostles, is it because we have a high opinion of ourselves and want to assume a position to rule over others, or is it because the Lord has sent us and given us the authority to do the work that He desires us to do? If we love to be first among the brothers and desire to rule over others, we are false apostles. However, if God has truly sent us and commissioned us, we are apostles. We are apostles and have authority only when we have God's commission.

The saints in the churches need to ask themselves regarding what they have received. A church cannot receive a work but reject the authority of the work. When a church receives a work, it has to receive the authority of the work. Once a church receives the authority of the work, those in the church must acknowledge that the person commissioned to carry out the work is an apostle. Once the saints are clear regarding who is an apostle and what are work and authority, they will be clear regarding the offices. Once the matter of apostles is made clear, the matter of elders and deacons will spontaneously be made clear.

Since the church has the authority of the Head, it is three-dimensional, not flat. In the local churches authority is not centralized. In Acts and the Epistles the churches of the Jews did not have authority over the churches of the Gentiles, nor did the churches of the Gentiles have authority over the churches of the Jews. The church in Antioch did not control the church in Jerusalem, nor did the church in Jerusalem control the church in Antioch. The church in Ephesus was mentioned first among the seven churches in Asia (Rev. 1:11), but it did not have authority to control other churches. In the

Bible there is not such a thing as a centralized authority among the churches; rather, all the local churches are directly under the authority of the Head. All the apostles are also directly under the authority of the Head.

If we are sent by the Lord to a certain place to participate in the work, we should not be proud or overly humble. Rather, we should have a deep consciousness that the Head has sent us and that the presence, the authority, of the Head is with us. There is no rank among the apostles. There are no superior apostles in the church. There is only the authority from the Head. Nevertheless, Timothy, Titus, Silas, and Silvanus labored under the apostle Paul because he perfected them. The places where they worked were places where Paul had worked. They were under Paul's leadership and carried out the same work (1 Tim. 1:2-3; Titus 1:4-5; Acts 15:40; 1 Thes. 1:1). However, we cannot say that Paul was under Peter or that Peter was under Paul. They were both directly appointed by the Lord to work in two different regions—the Jewish region and the Gentile region. Neither had any rank in relation to the other. If they had possessed rank in relation to one another, the result would have been a system of hierarchy as seen in the Roman Catholic Church.

In the way arranged by God, He will not let His authority suffer loss, and He will not allow human hands to act freely in His work. In other words, God desires that His authority be acknowledged in the church, and He prohibits men from acting freely. In God's work, if a person does not have a commission directly from the Head, he will lose the authority that comes directly from the Lord.

Although apostleship is a position, the position is not permanent. When a person is not commissioned by the Lord for a work, he does not have apostolic authority. This requires an apostle to always live in the Lord's commission. On the side of an apostle, the Lord sends him and commissions his work. On the side of the church, a church cannot receive the work of an apostle but not his authority, both of which are from the Lord. If this were the case, the saints would be without restriction. Even though some people are saved, they do not want to submit to God's authority. On the contrary, if we submit to authority, it will be easy for us to discern in our spirit whether or not a worker has the Lord's authority. When we exercise our spirit, we can easily discern whether a person has authority, that is, whether he submits to the Head and has been commissioned by the Head.

To Submit to an Apostle's Authority Being to Accept His Apostleship

In summary, an apostle is not appointed by man; rather, he is acknowledged by man. However, those who acknowledge an apostle do not become an authority to the apostle; rather, they submit to the apostle's authority. An apostle is one who absolutely submits himself to God and who receives his work and commission from the Lord. In the work an apostle receives a measure of authority, which enables him to carry out the work. Moreover, those who receive his work must accept his authority. To accept his authority is to acknowledge that he is an apostle. If there is a lack, it is proof that there are problems with the work and the church in that particular place. If these two aspects are not made clear, both the work and the church will be abnormal. For the work to be normal and the church to be strong, those sent by the Lord must be dealt with by the Lord, and those who receive the work must learn certain lessons before the Lord.

We may desire to receive a work, but are we willing to submit to authority? This is an important question. An apostle should ask himself whether he has authority when he goes out to work. Some people work without authority. We must remember that those who are not sent by the Lord but go out to work by themselves have only a work but no authority. On our part, we must do only one work—the work that the Lord has sent us to do. Then when we go out to work, we will go with authority. Moses was an apostle sent by God to bring the children of Israel out of the land of Egypt. When Moses led the children of Israel out of Egypt, he had not only a work but also authority. When the children of Israel caused trouble and even rebelled against him, he did not contend with them; instead, he turned to Jehovah God and spoke to Him of His work (cf. Exo. 32).

When the children of Israel worshipped the golden calf at the foot of Mount Sinai, God wanted to forsake them. He said to Moses, "Go, get down; for your people, whom you brought up out of the land of Egypt, have corrupted themselves" (v. 7). Moses replied, "Jehovah, why does Your anger burn against Your people, whom You brought out of the land of Egypt with great power and with a mighty hand?" (v. 11). God was angered by the children of Israel and wanted to destroy them, yet Moses immediately told Him that the children of Israel were *His* people, whom *He* had brought out of the land of Egypt. In other words, God, not Moses, brought the people out of the land of Egypt. What Moses meant was that God's people were God's business, not his. When we serve the Lord and encounter difficulties, can we be like Moses and boldly tell God, "God, this is Your work. This is Your business"?

There can be no pretension in this matter. If someone dares to pretend, God will strongly touch his conscience and ask him, "Whose work is this?" One who is sent by God for a particular work surely has received from God the authority inherent in his work. He who has the authority in the work must be commissioned by God. Man does not determine who has authority. However, if those who receive the work have been shown mercy by God and have learned the necessary lessons, they will know that authority is inherent in the work. If one does not receive authority, he will miss the blessing.

Some people speak of authority in the church so that they can control other people and make them submit to their personal authority. If this is the case, we had better not submit to such authority. Authority is not a tool to ensnare people; nonetheless, God's children cannot receive the work that God carries out through His servants, yet deny the authority that God has given to his servants. If we deny the authority of God in one of God's servants, we should utterly reject that person's work. This is permissible. However, if we desire to receive the work that God is carrying out through His servant, we should not deny His servant's authority.

If God's children are afraid to receive the authority of one of God's servants because they are afraid of being ensnared and controlled by someone who assumes to have authority, they should examine or test that person. They can do so by observing whether or not there is blessing related to the work. If we receive a work but reject the authority related to the work, our inner eyes will be blind and we will be in darkness; moreover, we will not have the blessing related to the work. God has established laws related to the universe and even laws related to our body. Likewise, God has also established laws in the church, the Body of Christ. One of these laws is that the Lord gives authority to the one whom He commissions to do His work. We cannot receive the work of one of God's servants yet reject his authority. If this is the case, we will surely lose the blessing.

Those who always say that the church is wrong and that the Lord's servants are wrong will never be able to rise up. Their eyes are blind. My point is that, logically speaking, these people should be clear and strong, because if they were not clear, how could they tell that others are wrong? Moreover, if they themselves are not strong, how can they continually condemn others? The fact is that the more they say that the church is wrong, the worse and the more abnormal they become.

If we meet a person who has not been meeting for half a year, we might expect him to say that the elders are wrong, the responsible brothers are wrong, and the workers are wrong. The only thing that he will be able to see is that everyone else is wrong. Why is it that the weakest one knows everyone else's shortcomings? This is because he has lost the blessing and does not see clearly. He has lost the blessing and does not have clear sight. This is because he has received God's work but has rejected the authority of the one who was commissioned with the work.

God has never given any person the authority to determine who is an apostle. Rather, apostleship can be acknowledged by the apostles themselves and by those who receive the apostles' work. Whether or not a person is an apostle is something that must be proven by the person himself and by those who receive his work. No one can control or determine anything by himself, because authority comes from the Lord's hand.

CHAPTER EIGHT

THE PRACTICE OF
THE ORGANIZATION OF THE CHURCH

(4)

A SUPPLEMENTARY WORD

In the organization of the church there is the need for both gifts and offices. Gifts are related to the Spirit, and offices are related to authority. Both are indispensable to the organization of the church. Most of the problems that have arisen throughout the ages in regard to the organization of the church are related to offices, not gifts. It is difficult to pretend to have a gift. If a person has a gift, he has a gift. If he does not have a gift, he does not have a gift. It is very clear. However, because man is involved in the appointing of some offices, it is not difficult to falsely claim to have an office. Since gifts do not involve the element of human appointment, there is not the problem of human mixture. With offices, however, there is the element of human appointment; hence, there is often human mixture.

The appointment of apostles is directly from God. No human hand is involved. The appointment of elders and deacons, however, involves the apostles' participation. The apostles who appoint elders and deacons must be fully subject to the authority of Christ the Head, and they must be governed by the Holy Spirit and led by the Holy Spirit. Whenever they appoint men to be elders and deacons, they fully represent the authority of the Head and should be under the authority of the Head. God carries out the appointment of elders and deacons in this way so that His authority in the church will not suffer loss, and there will be no confusion in the church. Consequently, no one can simply declare, "I am an elder" or "I am a deacon." If the brothers were free to do so, there would be much confusion in the church.

Suppose several thousand believers were meeting in several locations in Taipei. If some were not clearly appointed as elders and deacons, it would be hard to imagine their condition. However, in the appointment of elders and deacons, the apostles must let the Holy Spirit have the authority. Some like to say emphatically, "The Holy Spirit is the authority." On the surface, those who say this seem to be correct, but in their practice they still must make arrangements. One time, some brothers came to me and said, "In the church there should not be any arrangement; rather, we should give the Holy Spirit the absolute authority." This word is appealing to the ear, and I agree. Nevertheless, when I asked these brothers whether they arranged for someone to give messages and for others to lead the singing, they could not answer. If there are no arrangements, the chairs in the meeting hall will not be clean, and the bread and the cup will not be spread upon the table. Many times, those who use nice slogans do the very thing that they condemn.

Concerning honoring the authority of the Holy Spirit, no one can exceed Paul. Paul absolutely believed in the authority of the Holy Spirit, yet he still made certain arrangements. He said to the church in Corinth, "Whomever you approve, I will send them...and if it is fitting for me also to go, they will go with me. Now I will come to you when I pass through Macedonia, for I will pass through Macedonia. And perhaps I will stay with you, or even spend the winter, that you may send me forward wherever I may go. For I do not wish to see you now just in passing, for I am hoping to remain with you for some time, if the Lord permits" (1 Cor. 16:3-7). Moreover, he charged Timothy, "Be diligent to come to me quickly...The cloak which I left in Troas with Carpus, bring when you come, and the scrolls, especially the parchments" (2 Tim. 4:9, 13). Unlike some so-called spiritual people, Paul did not tell Timothy to first pray and see if he had the Lord's leading and to come only when he had the Lord's leading. According to these illustrations, it seems that we are more "spiritual" than Paul.

Every matter has two sides; we should not acknowledge one side and neglect the other. Elders must be appointed by men; otherwise, anyone would be free to rise up and claim, "I am an elder." When Samuel anointed David, Samuel's position was similar to that of an apostle, and David's position was similar to that of an elder. The authority to administrate was given to David by Samuel. However, it was really God who gave David authority through Samuel. Samuel performed the anointing, or appointment, yet he carried it out under God's authority. In regard to the organization in God's house, the church, we need to see that authority comes directly from the Head but that man also has a part. Authority comes directly from the Head. In this way the authority of the Head does not suffer loss. Man has a part in making the appointments in order to avoid confusion. Without human involvement in the appointment, there would be confusion. The story of the succession of David is the best illustration. If David had not appointed his son Solomon to succeed to his throne, the result would have been much confusion, because the other sons of David also desired to be king.

Even though David appointed Solomon, there was still a chaotic situation. This also happens in the church. Although an elder has been appointed, some may say, "Why should we submit to him? Is he qualified to be an elder?" This can be compared to the rising up of Solomon's brother Adonijah (1 Kings 1:5). The truth is of two sides, and we should never lean toward just one side. In order to avoid confusion, we must let the Head have the authority but also not neglect the human side.

Every genuine work is of the Lord, and behind every such work is His authority. We should not receive a work but deny the authority behind it. If we receive a work, we should recognize the authority behind it. To recognize this authority is to recognize the apostles. As those serving the Lord, we should all be able to say, "The Lord called me. He gave me a part in the work, and He has sent me to carry it out." Since the Lord has sent us to do the work, He surely has given us some authority. Even in a matter as small as sending someone to shop for groceries, the one sent must receive the authority to offer suggestions and make decisions.

Since the Lord has given us a part in the work, He must also have given us some authority. We should have the assurance that the Lord has sent us to do the work and that we have the authority to carry it out. We must bear in mind, however, that no serving one should do the work for himself. If a serving one works for himself, there will be problems. If he does not work for the Lord, the Lord will not acknowledge that his work is of the Lord or that he has been sent by the Lord. There will be no authority behind the work, and such a one will not be an apostle. Therefore, we need to ask ourselves, "Am I sent by the Lord? Am I working for the Lord? Is this the Lord's work?" If we can answer these questions in the affirmative, we should not only believe that we have the authority, but we should apply this authority in faith.

As far as an apostle is concerned, he has been given authority, and as far as the saints are concerned, those who receive help and supply from his work should also receive the authority behind the work. This is an unchanging principle. It would have been permissible for a saint in Jerusalem to not receive Paul as an apostle, if the saint had not received benefit from Paul's work. However, a saint from Corinth or Ephesus who heard Paul speak and received a supply from his work should not reject the authority related to Paul's work. Please remember, if we reject the authority of an apostle from whom we have received help, we are violating a great principle and will suffer a great loss. This is certain. May we be clear concerning this matter.

In the church no one can control others, and there is no ground to centralize authority in one place. Authority is with the Head. If someone is subject to the authority of the Head and has been commissioned by the Head for a part in the work, he will also receive authority from the Head. This authority is not given through any human hand. Upon receiving the work, he will sense that he has authority. When he carries out the work, he will be able to freely apply this authority. This cannot be controlled by anyone. This is the fellowship of the Body, the confirmation of the church, and it is under the authority of the Head. No one can control this. This is under the authority of the Head. Whoever is called by the Head to be an apostle, must be an apostle.

In Acts 13 when the five prophets and teachers in Antioch were, from a pure heart, seeking the Lord's will and desiring to give the Lord the opportunity to work freely, the Holy Spirit said to them that He would send two of them to carry out the work that He desired them to do. "As they were ministering to the Lord and fasting, the Holy Spirit said, Set apart for Me now Barnabas and Saul for the work to which I have called them" (vv. 1-2). As a result of the Spirit's sending, Barnabas and Saul went out with authority. They had the inward assurance that they were sent and commissioned by the Lord to carry out God's work. Hence, they had the confidence that in them there was authority. This is one side. On the other side, those who received their work knew and recognized them as apostles, knowing their work had ministered to them by either begetting or edifying them. All who acknowledge the work that they have received must bear in mind that all genuine work comes from the Lord and thus must have the Lord's authority behind it. If a work does not have the Lord's authority, it must not be of the Lord. If we receive a work, we also are receiving the Lord's authority behind it. If we receive the work but not the authority, we are violating a basic principle and will lose the blessing.

Some oppose and criticize other Christian groups yet are still able to pray and fellowship with God. However, those who receive an apostle's work will lose their sense of peace if they have problems with the apostle and doubt his authority. This is not something that we need to be told. We should all be clear regarding this point. For example, if a person on the street does something wrong and we speak ill of him, we may still have peace within, but if our parents do something wrong and we speak ill of them, we will become like Ham, who exposed his father's mistake. This led to a tragic end (Gen. 9:20-22, 25).

If we receive supply from an apostle, we need to receive his authority. No human being can appoint an apostle. The Lord has not handed over this matter to men. The apostles themselves must be assured of their own apostleship, and those who are edified by an apostle must acknowledge that he is an apostle. When an apostle's condition before the Lord becomes abnormal, he will lose his apostleship. Likewise, if those who receive supply from an apostle do not recognize his apostleship, he is no longer an apostle to them. Who is an apostle? On the side of an apostle, he is one who submits to God's authority, who is sent by the Head, and who is joined to the will of the Head to do the work that the Head desires him to do. Only the apostle can determine this. On the side of the saints, an apostle is one from whom they receive genuine edification and help; in other words, who they are as Christians is a result of his labor. Likewise, who we are as human beings is in large part due to our parents. Hence, when a saint recognizes the work, he should also recognize the apostle. This matter is not under anyone's control.

If we do not adequately fear the Lord or have much learning before the Lord, we may receive help from an apostle but not keep our position. Consequently, we may speak casually in judgment of his apostleship and may not consider him to be an apostle. On the other hand, if those who are apostles do not submit to the authority of God but do their own work, having their own future and ambition, they will lose their office as apostles. Hence, being an apostle depends on the apostle himself, whereas recognizing an apostle depends upon the recognizing one. Whether a person is an apostle is dependent upon his condition before the Lord, and whether a person receives another as an apostle is also dependent upon his condition before the Lord. This matter is not under any human control. We have to bow our heads and worship the Lord, saying, "O Lord, the authority is entirely in Your hands."

CHAPTER NINE

THE PRACTICE OF THE ORGANIZATION OF THE CHURCH

(5)

Elders and Deacons

Those Who Appoint Elders— the Apostles Who Submit to the Authority of the Holy Spirit

To be an elder or deacon in the church is a matter of office. To have an office is altogether related to authority. A person fulfills his office in the church by life and gifts, not by authority. However, his being appointed to an office is a matter of authority. The source of authority is Christ, the Head of the church. The Head appoints apostles in the church, and apostles, by the authority given to them from the Head, appoint elders and deacons in all the local churches. Hence, the appointment of elders and deacons is carried out through the authority of the apostles. The authority of the apostles is so definite that if an elder sins and the church is not able to solve the problem, the church should bring the accusation against the sinning elder to an apostle (1 Tim. 5:19), in the same manner as if they were going to court. This is because the apostles have authority over the elders.

In many organizations in today's society, members have the right both to elect and to recall those responsible for the organization. In the church, however, the appointment of elders is not in the hands of the saints but in the hands of God or, we can say, in the hands of the apostles who were appointed by the Head. The apostles' appointment of the elders is more than ninety percent based on life. Only a small portion is based on the elders' functions, or gifts.

We need to see that the appointment of elders and deacons is a matter of authority. If a local church could elect or recall elders, it would not be a normal church; rather, there would be confusion and degradation in the church. I hope that when we consider the church, we will not bring in the secular thought. Secular governments, regardless of size, are either autocracies or democracies. In the church, however, there is neither autocracy nor democracy but theocracy. The government of the church is neither an autocracy, rule by a single person, nor a democracy, rule by the people. Regardless of whether there is autocracy or democracy, the source is the same. Both are from man.

The government of the church is of God and from God. An apostle is qualified to appoint elders because he submits to the authority of the Head. The safeguard for the apostles is to live in the Holy Spirit and before the Head. Whenever an apostle, who has been appointed by the Head, fails to live in the Holy Spirit or before the Head, he loses the safeguard. The church then falls into human hands. The safeguard of authority in the government of the church lies in the apostles' living in the Holy Spirit and before the Head. In other words, if the apostles do not live in the Holy Spirit and before the Head, they should not appoint elders and deacons in the church.

I hope that those among us who take the lead in serving the Lord will be aware of this matter. If they do not live under the rule of the Holy Spirit and submit to the authority of the Head, they should not touch the eldership. If they touch this matter, the church will fall under the government of man and not be under God's government. The church should not be governed by man but by God. In order to avoid confusion, God has arranged a way to raise up some; that is, He has given apostles authority to appoint elders. If we consider this matter calmly, we will realize that God's way is excellent. This way requires the church to be spiritual, and it also requires that those in the church, including the apostles, elders, and deacons, be spiritual. If the saints are not spiritual, they will not fear God or submit to the authority of the Head, nor will they receive the elders and deacons.

If an apostle does not live in the Holy Spirit or before the Head, he loses his position to appoint elders. If he does things according to his own will and acts on his own accord, even though he may continue to serve, he does not have the authority to appoint elders. The authority to appoint elders is with the Holy Spirit. Only when an apostle lives in the Holy Spirit and submits to the authority of the Head can he receive authority from the Head. Only then can he exercise authority to appoint elders. God used the prophet Samuel to anoint kings, because Samuel was such a prophet. It is not sufficient to be merely a prophet. To anoint a king, a prophet must be like Samuel. Eli could not anoint a king because he had lost God's presence (1 Sam. 2:27-36). Hence, not everyone who was called a prophet could establish the kingship. In order to be qualified to anoint someone as king, a prophet had to be like Samuel; that is, he had to live under God's authority and receive God's command. In the same way, to be qualified to appoint elders, an apostle must be one who lives under the authority of God, is ruled by the Holy Spirit, and receives the Holy Spirit's command.

The appointing of elders in a local church is a crucial matter. It matters a great deal whether or not a person is in the Holy Spirit or outside of the Holy Spirit. There is not a rule or principle that states, "It is the serving ones who appoint elders, and since some of the serving ones are apostles, they should appoint elders." Rather, it is the authority of the Head that appoints elders. Strictly speaking, it is not the apostles, but the authority of the Holy Spirit that appoints elders. When an apostle is about to appoint an elder, he must first ask himself whether he has the authority of the Holy Spirit and whether he is submitting to the authority of the Holy Spirit. This is a very important question. I am afraid that in some local churches, the appointment of the elders is not carried out under the authority of the Holy Spirit but according to rules and principles. If this is the case, there will not be the confirmation of the anointing in the appointment. Therefore, the appointing one must live in the Spirit.

The Qualifications of the Elders and Deacons

Submitting to the Authority of the Holy Spirit

There are several high spiritual requirements related to the offices in the church. The first requirement is that the appointing one must be in the Holy Spirit. If he is not in the Holy Spirit, even if he were the top apostle, he should not appoint elders. This is the requirement on the side of the appointing one. As for the appointed ones, that is, the elders and deacons, there are also spiritual requirements. In making an appointment, an apostle should not consider a person's position, reputation, ability, or wealth; instead, he should consider whether or not this person submits to the authority of the Head, that is, the authority of the Holy Spirit. To appoint an elder based on his position, reputation, ability, and wealth is certainly of men and not of God. In the church the appointing of an elder should always be a fearful matter. Position, reputation, ability, and wealth should never be considered; rather, all these matters must be put aside.

In order for one to be an overseer or an elder, the prerequisite is that he submit to the authority of the Head. If he does not submit to the authority of God, no one should put the responsibility for a local church into his hands. This is equivalent to asking Saul to be king instead of letting Jehovah God be King (1 Sam. 8—10). This is not acceptable. Biblical knowledge, ability to serve, and capability in handling matters are not the qualifications of an elder. Eldership is the first office in a local church. In the appointment of an elder, the first matter to be settled is whether or not a person submits to the authority of God.

I was not clear about this matter twenty years ago, but now the Lord has made us clear. To be an elder in the church is a matter of authority. Until the matter of authority is established and settled within a person, he cannot be an elder in the church. In Matthew 8 the centurion knew that he was a man under authority, that he was under some and that others were under him (v. 9). Only a person who knew and submitted to authority could be a centurion. Likewise, only one who knows the authority of God can be an elder. Consider the example of David. He could manage God's house because he was a man according to God's heart; he allowed God to reign through him and by him. The thing we fear the most is that an elder would be like Saul, who reigned by himself and set God aside.

Do not think that David's honoring of Saul as God's anointed meant that Saul was proper before God. This was not the case. Similarly, an elder should not think that his position is proper simply because the saints regard him as an elder. Actually, the saints may regard him as an elder in the church because they have personally learned from God to submit to authority. Their regarding him as an elder does not vindicate him. On his side, an elder must be clear that he is under the authority of God. On the side of the appointing one, he should observe the one being appointed to see if he is under the authority of God and if the matter of authority has been settled within him.

No one who disobeys the authority of God can be God's deputy authority. No one who disobeys the authority of God can exercise God's authority in the church as an apostle and appoint elders. Whenever we consider the matter of authority in others, the Holy Spirit also checks with us to see if the matter of authority is settled in us. Hence, we have to see that the matter of office in the church is altogether a matter of authority. For example, when an apostle is about to appoint an elder, the first thing he needs to consider is whether the matter of authority is settled in the one being considered for appointment. As the apostle considers this person, the Holy Spirit will also ask him if the matter of authority is settled within him. If the matter of authority is not settled within an apostle, he certainly is not qualified to consider whether it is settled in others. The government of the church is God's government; that is, it is under the authority of the Holy Spirit. If no one in the church submits to the authority of the Holy Spirit, it will be impossible to have elders and unnecessary to appoint some. To do so would only produce a few more Sauls. Hence, a strict requirement in regard to the appointing of elders is that the one being appointed must submit to the authority of God.

Experienced in Life

Another basic requirement for elders is related to the matter of life. The designation *elder* implies life. One who is not sufficiently mature in life cannot be an elder, because to be an elder is a matter of life. One who is older surely has a considerable measure of life. When the apostles appoint an elder, they should first consider his condition before God with regard to authority; second, they should consider his condition in life. Strictly speaking, an elder is not the result of an appointment but is produced by growth in life.

Our eyes must be opened to see that education, ability, reputation, position, and wealth are not qualifications to be considered in the appointment of elders. Whenever the apostles take these things into consideration in their appointing of elders, this indicates that the church has degraded and is no longer under the authority of the Holy Spirit. In appointing elders, an apostle should consider only two principal matters: authority and life. However, the degree to which an elder should be experienced in life is not absolute but relative. A person may be qualified to be an elder in a small local church, one that is newly raised up, but he may not be qualified to be an elder in a larger church, one that has more experience in life.

Having Functions

In the appointing of elders, the two crucial matters to consider are the matters of authority and life. Once these two matters are clear, there can be an additional consideration, that is, how much function a brother has. If two persons are similar in their submission to authority and in their condition of life, yet one has a greater function than the other, then the one with the greater function should be appointed. In the appointment of elders one should pay attention to function, but function is not a crucial matter. What is truly important are the matters of authority and life. Because the elders submit to authority, they are qualified to represent authority in the church. The elders are the authority in a local church. The reason they can be the authority is that they themselves submit to authority. A person who does not submit to authority is not qualified to be an authority. If I am under some people, and some are under me, my being under them is a matter of my submitting to authority, and some being under me is a matter of my being the authority.

The degree to which an elder submits to God's authority will be the degree to which people submit to him as an authority. When the children of Israel rose up against Moses, he did not say, "I have authority, and I will strike you down." On the contrary, when the children of Israel troubled him, he prostrated himself before God. As a result, God spoke on his behalf and defended him. Today God's speaking and defending take place in others' spirits. It is not an outward matter. The Spirit of God in the spirit of others causes them to submit. The saints' submission to an elder is based on the elder's submission to God. Strictly speaking, the authority is not the elder, nor is it something of his own. The authority is God, and it belongs to God. The key is whether or not an elder submits to the authority of God.

Some may be concerned about others assuming authority, but it must be understood that nothing is more real and more difficult to feign than authority. If a person submits to the authority of the Holy Spirit, he does not need to boast and say, "I submit to the authority of God." When others contact him, they can sense whether or not he has authority. However, if he does not submit to the authority of God, no matter how much he tries to assume authority and declares himself an authority, his efforts will be useless. When others contact him, they will be able to discern the real situation. Saul is Saul, and David is David. Whenever we contact others, they know whether we are David or Saul. In regard to authority, a person simply cannot pretend. Submission to authority is a serious requirement for the elders.

The Appointment of Elders and Its Relationship to the Condition of the Saints

There Must Be Spiritual Saints in Order to Have Spiritual Elders

In regard to the appointment of elders, the saints also face a serious requirement; that is, they must be spiritual. Any time the saints do not submit to the authority of God and are not proper in their inward condition toward God, they will choose Saul and reject David. However, if they submit to God, and are proper in their inward condition toward God, they will choose David and reject Saul. When an elder who is in the flesh meets with a believer who is in the flesh, they will either talk nicely or argue fiercely. The flesh is able to be friendly or quarrelsome.

The kind of elder a saint prefers shows the kind of person the saint is. Those who are deceived by fleshly elders are surely in the flesh themselves. This can be compared to a person who becomes sick. When the body is weak, germs invade; however, if the body is strong, it is hard for germs to invade. Therefore, never say that an elder has deceived you. If you have been deceived, this shows not only that he is living in the flesh but also that you are living in the flesh.

The kind of kings whom the children of Israel preferred was an indication of their condition. The fact that they wanted Saul to be king shows that they were like Saul. When saints in a church are fleshly, we should not expect the elders among them to be spiritual. Even if the elders were spiritual, they would feel a need to be somewhat hidden. At such a time someone like Saul, who has a big stature, would surely rise up to lead them as king. He would do so because there are many fleshly ones to support him, and it would be the best opportunity for him to be enthroned.

In contrast, when the saints learn to live in the spirit and submit to God's authority, there will be absolutely no place for Saul. If a Saul rises up, the spiritual atmosphere will certainly subdue him, and he will not be given any ground. Then a David, a man according to God's heart, will rise up and reign for God. Hence, the condition of the elders in the church speaks forth the condition of the church. In other words, the condition of the church testifies of the condition of the elders in the church. A spiritual church will have spiritual elders. In the same way, the presence of spiritual elders indicates that the church is spiritual.

For the Glory and Beauty of the Church to Be Manifested, the Apostles, Elders, and Saints All Needing to Be Spiritual

The apostles who appoint elders must be spiritual, and those who are appointed to be elders must also be spiritual. Moreover, the saints who receive the elders' authority must be spiritual too. All three must be spiritual. Authority in the church is not a matter of autocracy or democracy but theocracy. The problem in many churches is that those who appoint the elders, the appointed ones, and those who receive the appointed elders are not spiritual. Nevertheless, all say that they do things according to biblical principles. May we all be clear that biblical principles are not a guarantee of being spiritual. Only the authority of the Holy Spirit can safeguard us and cause us to be genuinely spiritual.

Biblical principles can be living only if they are applied in the Holy Spirit; otherwise, they are merely dead letters. If an apostle is going to appoint an elder, he must ask himself whether or not he is in the Holy Spirit. Likewise, if a brother is about to be appointed as an elder, he needs to ask himself whether or not he is in the Holy Spirit. Moreover, when a saint receives someone as an elder, an authority, the saint should ask himself whether or not he is in the Holy Spirit. If those who appoint elders, those who are appointed elders, and those who receive the elders are all in the Holy Spirit, others will see God's authority, God's government, in the church, and there will be a free way for the authority of the Head to be realized in the church.

Psalm 133:2-3 says, "It is like the fine oil upon the head / That ran down upon the beard, / Upon Aaron's beard, / That ran down upon the hem of his garments; / Like the dew of Hermon / That came down upon the mountains of Zion. / For there Jehovah commanded the blessing: / Life forever." In this psalm we see the dew, the oil, and Jehovah's commanded blessing, which is, life forever. This is the condition of Mount Zion, the condition of the mysterious Body of Christ. In other words, under this kind of condition, the glory and beauty of the church are fully expressed.

Sometimes in our fallen mind, questions may arise, "Is the church being controlled by someone? Are we being controlled?" When such questions arise within us, we should not consider the ones who appoint elders or the ones who are appointed elders; rather, we should consider ourselves and ask, "Where am I? Am I in the Holy Spirit or in the flesh?" If we are living in the Holy Spirit, no one can deceive or control us, and we will certainly know the condition of the ones who appoint elders. At the same time, we will also know the condition of the ones who have been appointed elders. Our safeguard does not lie in biblical principles but in the authority of the Holy Spirit.

If those who appoint elders, those who are appointed elders, and those who receive the elders all live according to the self, the church will be under the control of men. Although those in the church may say, "We are walking according to biblical principles," they have no life and have lost the safeguard of the Holy Spirit. To live in submission to the authority of the Holy Spirit is to obey the Spirit, not to walk merely according to the Bible. The administration of the church is safeguarded when everyone submits to the Spirit. When everyone submits to the Spirit, no one can pretend, nor can anyone deceive or control others. A person who submits to authority does not want to rule over others. The more spiritual authority a person has, the less he desires to rule over others. This is a wonderful matter. In contrast, all those who desire to rule over others do not submit to God's authority and do not have God's authority.

A person who does not submit to God's authority cannot deceive those who do. If we live under the authority of the Holy Spirit, we will know whether a person is living in submission to God's authority. We will know whether he is a Saul or a David, and we will not be deceived or controlled by him. If you say that someone has deceived you or exercised control over you, this indicates that both are living in the same place—the flesh. Living in the flesh is contagious. However, if an elder is the flesh and you are a living stone, the contagious infection will not affect you.

If we stay in the Spirit, we should not be worried about

anything, because the Holy Spirit is our safeguard. A person who lives in the flesh and according to his own will is a Saul. This will be very clear in the spirit of the saints. The Holy Spirit will speak, make known, and impart some feeling into the saints. The administration of the church is altogether a matter of God's government, of the authority of the Head, and of life. If we stay in the Spirit, the church surely will be spiritual and strong.

Similarly, the appointment of deacons is also a matter of authority. A person does not become a deacon simply because he desires to be one or because a group of brothers has nominated him. This requires the appointing by the apostles and is altogether a matter of the authority of the Head.

CHAPTER TEN

THE PRACTICE OF THE ORGANIZATION OF THE CHURCH

(6)

CONCERNING GIFTS

The Significance of Gifts

In existence and expression, the church has two aspects: a universal aspect and a local aspect. In administration and spiritual building up, the church has offices and gifts. *Gifts* is a specialized term. It refers to such abilities as speaking as a prophet, healing sicknesses, casting out demons, or speaking in tongues. The Greek word for *gift* refers to something that is given freely to someone else. Romans 6:23, which uses the word *gift,* says, "The gift of God is eternal life in Christ Jesus our Lord." The root of the word *gift* is very close to the word *grace;* hence, gift is a matter of grace. Gifts are given through grace. In other words, God solemnly gives us something without our paying a price. He freely bestows it upon us. This is a gift. A gift is not sold; it is given freely.

All gifts, whether they are for the church or for individuals, whether they are ordinary or miraculous, are given freely by God in grace to men. God gives gifts freely without requiring anything in return.

Gifts Being a Matter of Grace
The Source of Gifts Being Grace

Offices are a matter of authority, whereas gifts are a matter of grace. Offices depend on authority; gifts depend on grace. Offices are appointed through authority; gifts are given through grace. If a person is not under authority, he will not have an office. If a person loses grace, he will not have a gift. Even though gifts are a matter of grace, there is still a distinction between gifts and grace. Grace is the source of gifts. Although some people may lose grace, they may continue to possess a gift. This is an abnormal condition. The normal condition is that every gift should be of grace.

The Significance of Grace

Grace is the source of gifts, but what is grace? Generally speaking, this question is difficult to answer. Nevertheless, through our study in the past few years, many saints should have a better understanding of this matter. In simple terms, grace is God giving Himself to us. John 1:1 says, "In the beginning was the Word, and the Word was with God, and the Word was God." Then verse 14 says, "The Word became flesh and tabernacled among us...full of grace and reality." Then verse 16 continues, "For of His fullness we have all received, and grace upon grace." Based upon these words, we must confess that grace is God Himself.

All things and all matters in the universe are false. Only God Himself is real. The Bible never speaks of the good things and positive matters of this age as being grace. At most they are called the good things or blessings (Josh. 23:15; Jer. 18:10; Ezek. 44:30). In the Bible *grace* is a special term.

In 1 Corinthians 15:10 Paul said, "By the grace of God I am what I am; and His grace unto me did not turn out to be in vain, but, on the contrary, I labored more abundantly than all of them, yet not I but the grace of God which is with me." What was the grace that was with the apostle Paul? It was the God gained and experienced by Paul. He was able to labor more abundantly than the other apostles because he gained and experienced God who was in him. The apostle often ended his Epistles with similar words. Philippians 4:23 says, "The grace of the Lord Jesus Christ be with your spirit." Grace is with our spirit. This grace, which is with our human spirit, is the God whom we receive in our spirit. Simply put, grace in the New Testament is God Himself—that is, the Spirit of God, the life of God—being received by us. Second Timothy 2:1 says,

"You therefore, my child, be empowered in the grace which is in Christ Jesus." This grace is God received by us.

The grace spoken of in the New Testament is God; that is, God giving Himself, His Spirit, and His life to us for us to receive as grace. If we compare John 10, 14, 15, and 16 to chapter 1, we will see that God Himself is grace and that grace is the life of God, the Holy Spirit of God. John 1:14 says, "The Word became flesh and tabernacled among us...full of grace and reality." John 10:10 says, "I have come that they may have life." This shows that life is equivalent to grace. Moreover, 16:7 says, "It is expedient for you that I go away; for if I do not go away, the Comforter will not come to you; but if I go, I will send Him to you." The Comforter is the Holy Spirit. After resurrecting, the Lord came into the midst of the disciples and breathed into them, saying, "Receive the Holy Spirit" (20:22). Thus, the Holy Spirit is grace, God Himself, and God's life, which is spoken of in chapter 1. Hence, the Holy Spirit of God whom we receive is grace.

Two Verses That Speak of the Relationship between Gifts and Grace

In the New Testament two verses speak of the relationship between gifts and grace. The first verse is Ephesians 4:7, which says, "To each one of us grace was given according to the measure of the gift of Christ." This word is marvelous. The grace we receive is according to the measure of the gift. In other words, the amount of grace a person receives is according to the measure of the gift given to him. Gift is like a glass, and grace is like water. The amount of water that a glass can contain depends on the capacity of the glass. If the capacity of the glass is one cup, the amount of water it can receive is one cup. Thus, if a glass is large, it can receive a great amount of water, but if a glass is small, it can receive only a small amount. How much water that can come into the glass depends upon the capacity of the glass. In like manner, how much grace that we can receive is according to the gift that God has measured to us.

The second verse is Romans 12:6, which says, "Having gifts that differ according to the grace given to us." The gifts that we receive are according to the grace given to us. Ephesians says that grace is given according to the gift, but Romans says that gifts differ according to grace. The relationship between gift and grace is of two sides. The two are inseparable. Whether it is grace given according to gift or gift given according to grace, in either case the two cannot be separated. Once a person loses grace, he loses any related gift. If a person loses grace but still exercises his gift, his exercise of the gift will be abnormal. The normal condition of a gift is altogether in grace.

Explanations of the Two Verses

Gifts Being Received according to Grace

Although we spoke first of Ephesians 4 and then Romans 12, according to sequence Romans 12 comes before Ephesians 4. First, Romans speaks of gifts being according to grace, then Ephesians speaks of grace being according to gifts. When we are saved, God first gives grace, not gifts; that is, God imparts Himself into us. Grace is God Himself—the life of God, the Spirit of God—and this is what God gives to us first. When God saves us, He gives Himself to us as life and as the Spirit. As a result, we have grace within us. Before we were saved, we had only sins and were empty within. Now that we are saved, we have grace within and are no longer empty. Upon being saved, God Himself—God's life and God's Spirit—came in. God, as life and Spirit, is grace to us.

According to Romans 12, God gives us gifts according to grace and based on grace. Hence, the gifts in Romans 12 are given according to grace. God's life, God's Spirit, and God Himself become grace in man. Grace is the basis. Out of grace come gifts. Within is grace, and without are gifts. The grace we receive is the same, but the gifts manifested in us differ. In some the gift of love is manifested, in others the giving of hospitality is manifested, and in still others the ministry of the word is manifested. It may be easy for us to understand that the ministry of the word is a gift, but it is probably difficult to understand that giving hospitality is also a gift.

The most difficult thing for some Christians is to give

hospitality. Some saints are willing to do whatever the brothers ask of them, except give hospitality. Giving hospitality is too troublesome. In the church, in the past there was always the practice of giving hospitality among the saints. In recent years, however, the saints seem to have lost this grace. Thus, they have also lost the gift. Nevertheless, there are some who having received God's grace are not only willing to give hospitality but also consider it the sweetest matter. In this way, giving hospitality has become their gift. From this we see that gifts are produced out of grace and are given to us according to the grace within us.

Even though gifts may differ, they are the result of the same grace. This can be compared to the circulation of blood in our body. When blood flows to the ears, it enables them to hear. When blood flows to the eyes, it helps them to see, and when blood flows to the mouth, it enables the mouth to speak. However, if the blood circulation stops, almost immediately the ears cannot hear, the eyes cannot see, and the mouth cannot speak. There is only one circulation of blood, but when it flows to different places, it enables different functions to be manifested. Similarly, everyone has the same grace, but the gifts manifested within them are different. We all have received the same grace, but the gifts that are manifested through us are different.

Paul received a large measure of grace. According to Old Testament typology, the grace that Paul received can be compared to a large bull. In contrast, we may have received only a small amount of grace. According to Old Testament typology, the grace that we have received may be equivalent only to a small pigeon. It is the same grace, but its measure is different. Hence, the gifts that are produced by this grace are also different. The main point is that gifts result from grace. We cannot expect someone without God's life and God's Spirit to have a gift. Only a person who has the life of God has a gift. Of course, in the Old Testament age it was a different matter. In the New Testament everyone who has a gift has life and grace.

Gifts Being Sustained in Grace

Gifts are given according to and based upon the grace

within. After a person has a gift, God needs to continue to supply that person with grace. This is what is spoken of in Ephesians 4. Grace is according to the measure of the gift. The Lord gives a person grace, produces a gift within him, and then supplies grace according to the gift in him. If a person's gift is great, God will supply him continually with a great amount of grace. If his gift is small, God will supply him continually with a small amount of grace. Thus, grace is given according to the measure of the gift. In order to exercise our gift, we need the supply of grace.

All those who minister the word can testify that they need a great supply of grace from God. Although to minister the word is not necessarily a great gift, neither is it a small gift. Hence, it requires much grace from God. It would be terrible if God gave us gifts without supplying us continually with grace. If God gave us ears but did not give us a supply of blood, our ears would be useless. Moreover, if the blood supplied to our shoulders was only equal to the supply to our ears, it would not be possible for the shoulders to function. The shoulders need much blood in order to function properly. Grace abounds in us according to the gifts that we have received. Grace is given to us according to the measure of our gifts.

The strength for a person to minister the word depends entirely on the inward anointing, supply of life, and presence of God—all of which are grace. I can testify that when I speak for the Lord, I am not afraid of not having anything to say. What I am afraid of is that when I am speaking, I may not be able to touch God inwardly. This is the most awful thing. If grace is gone, God is gone, and nothing is left within. It is most terrible for the inward source to be cut off and for there to be no supply of grace. However, it is wonderful when a person who has been appointed as God's mouthpiece opens his mouth and the supply within him begins to flow. As long as he is ministering the word for God, the grace and supply within him will come. The grace given by God to each one is according to the measure of the gift that he has received.

Gifts Being a Matter of Life and Spirituality

Offices are a matter of authority, that is, of submitting

ourselves to God. Gifts are a matter of grace, that is, of touching God, living in fellowship with God, and having the presence of God, the life supply, and the anointing. Gifts are produced from grace, and when we exercise our gifts, we need the supply of grace. Romans tells us that gifts come from grace, and Ephesians tells us that we need the supply of grace in order to exercise our gifts. Hence, we need grace both in the receiving of gifts and in the exercise of gifts. Without grace, there is no gift. If we have gifts but are without a continual supply of grace, we will not be able to exercise our gifts. The producing of gifts requires grace, and the exercise of gifts also requires grace. Gifts are produced and exercised through grace, and grace is related to life. Hence, when we touch life and exercise our gifts, all the problems are solved.

Offices are a matter of authority, and gifts are a matter of spirituality. Spirituality is a matter of grace, that is, a matter of life. Every gift comes from life, from the Spirit. The Spirit is the realization of God's life. Hence, only by living constantly in grace and in the anointing can one be spiritual. Grace and spirituality are inseparable.

If a saint constantly lives in fellowship with the Lord and is continually experiencing the supply of life and the anointing, a gift will surely be manifested in him. In contrast, if a person ceases to experience grace and loses his fellowship with the Lord, he will have no anointing, no supply, and no manifestation of gift. If a brother is weak and depressed, his function will not be manifested. However, once he is enlivened, the gift within him will immediately be manifested without his having received any teaching. Formerly, he may not have been willing to give hospitality, but after praying and contacting the Lord, he may have the burden and willingness to pay the price and to joyfully provide hospitality to saints from afar.

Likewise, a brother may cease meeting for a long period of time and have no inward fellowship with the Lord. Being severed from grace, He does not have a heart to love the Lord. Although He may attend meetings occasionally, he does so out of duty and has absolutely no heart for the service or administration of the church. One day, however, he may touch the

Lord inwardly, receive grace, and be revived. Later, when he stands up in a meeting and gives a testimony, many saints may have a response in their spirit, saying, "This brother will one day be an elder." Even though he was revived only recently, his gift, that is, his care for people and for the church, his insight, and his orderly handling of matters may immediately be manifested. In other words, the brother definitely has a gift, and this gift comes from grace.

Another brother, after being saved for five years, may not be clear regarding spiritual matters; however, he may be able to speak clearly and reasonably about many secular topics, including philosophy, aesthetics, politics, or economics. One day he may touch the Lord in a meeting and receive grace. Three weeks later he may give a testimony in a meeting. Upon hearing him speak, many may sense that he has the gift of ministering the word. Even though his testimony is about how he was saved and gained by the Lord, his speaking is nonetheless an excellent message that inspires people. He is able to do this because he has enjoyed grace and has a gift for ministering the word.

Gifts come from grace. In the church even sweeping the floor is a gift. When we live in grace, it is impossible not to manifest the gifts that we have received (Rom. 12). For instance, when a person touches the Lord, he may receive grace to wipe the windows and to clean the meeting hall on the Lord's Day morning. The reason he does these things is not that certain ones have asked him to; rather, he does these things because of the gift within him. If he does not function according to his gift, he will feel uneasy for the entire week. This is a gift.

Grace enables us to manifest our gifts; thus, we should never forget that we need a continual supply of grace in order to exercise these gifts. According to Ephesians 4, the amount of grace we receive depends entirely on the measure of gift we have received.

CONCLUSION

We cannot speak of the organization of the church apart from God's authority and God's grace. Without God's authority and grace, there is a lack in the organization of the church.

All that is left is a social group, a societal organization, not the genuine church with a proper organization. The organization of the church is under God's authority and in God's grace. If we do not submit to God's authority and are not enjoying God's grace, we should not speak of the organization of the church. In its essence the organization of the church is based on God's authority and God's grace. Offices come from His authority, and gifts come from His grace. Everyone who fulfills his office submits to God's authority; everyone who exercises his gift lives in grace. This is the organization of the church.

When we carry out our offices in the church, we must ask ourselves whether or not we are submitting to God's authority and whether or not we are living in fellowship with God. If we do not submit to God or live in fellowship with God, whatever we do will be worthless, even if it is scriptural. It will be nothing but human organization. It is not sufficient to measure ourselves only according to biblical principles. If we are not under God's authority and experiencing God's grace, even though we may be doing things according to biblical principles, all that we have is human organization. We need to be rescued from such a situation.

In the past many saints held firmly to biblical principles without realizing the significance of authority and grace. To speak about the organization of the church according to the letter in the Bible will produce merely another human organization. No matter how scriptural our practice may be, if it is only according to letter, it will still be human organization. In contrast, if we submit to God's authority and experience His grace, the condition among us will be according to the intrinsic principles of the Bible, even if our knowledge of the Bible is inadequate. Our being according to biblical principle is not a matter of letter or doctrine but a matter of spirit and life.

If we submit to God's authority in regard to the offices and experience God's grace in regard to the gifts, all the problems will be gone, and there will be no need for argument. In contrast, if we do not submit to God's authority or experience God's grace but are merely according to the principle of the letter in the Bible, sooner or later we will have disputes, and problems will arise among us. For the past century this has been the problem among the Brethren. May the Lord have mercy on us that we would never decide the matters of the organization of the church based merely on the letter in the Scriptures. We must see that the source of the organization of the church is God's authority and God's grace.

First Corinthians 12:4-5 says, "There are distinctions of gifts, but the same Spirit; and there are distinctions of ministries, yet the same Lord." *Spirit* denotes grace, and *Lord* denotes authority. The basic matters in the organization of the church are authority and grace. To have an office we must submit to authority, and to have a gift we must experience grace. Whenever we touch the organization of the church, we touch the authority of the Head and the grace of God.

May the Lord rescue us from being right in principle but dead in practicality. In this way, may we be His living Body, coordinating together, standing in our proper place, and supplying others according to our measure. This is the condition described in Psalm 133: "Behold, how good and how pleasant it is / For brothers to dwell in unity! / It is like the fine oil upon the head / That ran down upon the beard, / Upon Aaron's beard, / That ran down upon the hem of his garments; / Like the dew of Hermon / That came down upon the mountains of Zion. / For there Jehovah commanded the blessing: / Life forever."

SUPPLEMENTARY MESSAGES REGARDING CERTAIN MATTERS IN THE CHURCH THAT REQUIRE OUR ATTENTION

THE OUTLINE

I. There being no organizational unification among the churches:
   A. The examples in the Bible.
   B. Two dangers.
   C. Not having organizational unification:
      1. Not being unified in the move of the work.
      2. Not being unified in finance.
      3. Not having a central church or person.
   D. The proper attitude:
      1. Not being individualistic or loose.
      2. Needing to seek confirmation.
II. Some matters related to full-time service:
   A. Serving full time being a matter of commission:
      1. Everyone needing to serve.
      2. Serving full time being based on the Lord's commission.
   B. Needing to learn how to do things.
   C. Giving all the brothers and sisters an opportunity to serve.
   D. The question of financial support.
   E. Character and disposition.
III. Knowing the spiritual aspect of the church:
   A. The church being in resurrection:
      1. The experience of resurrection.
      2. The way to experience resurrection.
   B. The church being spiritual:
      1. Resurrection and the Holy Spirit being inseparable.
      2. The church existing only in the Holy Spirit.

C. The church being heavenly:
      1. The church being heavenly according to its nature.
      2. Heaven being related to the authority of God.
      3. To be heavenly being to submit to the authority of God.
      4. The heavenly condition of the church.
IV. Receiving people in the churches:
   A. An explanation of the fact and the principle.
   B. Two aspects of salvation—believing and being baptized.
   C. What man obtains through believing.
   D. Baptism being based upon the faith one already has.
   E. Needing to touch a person's inner feeling when receiving him.

CHAPTER ONE

THERE BEING NO ORGANIZATIONAL UNIFICATION AMONG THE CHURCHES

THE EXAMPLES IN THE BIBLE

There should be oneness but no unification among the churches. The condition of the Roman Catholic Church today is that of unification. The word *catholic* means "universal" and denotes a kind of universal unification. According to God's word, God does not desire that the churches be unified. In the first twelve chapters of Acts, Peter was the leading figure. As such, he was in constant fellowship with different churches. However, in these chapters there is no indication of unification among the churches in Judea. The churches in Judea were one and in one accord, yet they were not unified. They were one in service and in faith, but they were not unified. The Bible does not speak of unification. Although apostles are extra-local and have been entrusted by God to take care of multiple local churches, there should be no unification among those churches.

According to the record in the second half of Acts, from chapter 13 onward, Paul took the lead in the work. He took care of the church in Ephesus, the church in Antioch, the church in Corinth, and the churches in many other places; nevertheless, there is no record of unification among the churches under his care. Not only was there no such unification in practice; there was not even a hint of this kind of unification. In other words, Peter did not unify the churches in Judea, and Paul did not unify the churches among the Gentiles. Among the churches in the Jewish and Gentile regions, the flow was one, and the Spirit was one. There was oneness and one accord among them, but there was no unification. We need to be very careful in this matter.

TWO DANGERS

We face two dangers. On the one hand, as soon as there is unification among churches, the presence of the Holy Spirit is lost, and the work of the Holy Spirit is limited. On the other hand, if we think that we can be careless and free because there is no unification, we will fall into the flesh, and all our actions will be out of the self. Unification causes us to lose the power of the Holy Spirit and the opportunity for the Holy Spirit to work. However, ignoring our oneness because there is no unification causes us to become unruly and to fall into a fleshly situation. These are the two dangers that we face.

NOT HAVING ORGANIZATIONAL UNIFICATION

Not Being Unified in the Move of the Work

What does it mean to not have unification? We can explain this by using a few illustrations. For instance, for the past three years the brothers in Taiwan and the brothers overseas have been fellowshipping with me, hoping that some brothers from Taiwan could go to various places in Southeast Asia to work for the Lord in order to meet the need in these places. When I heard about the need, my heart was moved, but I did not feel at ease within. I was not sure why, but because of the uneasy feeling within, we have not dared to take any action, even though the need still exists.

Through spending time in the Lord's presence, we realized that this uneasy feeling was due to the danger of producing unification among the churches. If we were to send some brothers from Taiwan to various places in Southeast Asia, we would run the risk of producing a practice of unification. However, if some saints from Taipei, Kaohsiung, Taichung, or Hong Kong were to develop a burden within and a feeling that the Lord was calling them and commissioning them to go to Southeast Asia, whether it be one person or several people, we would bow our heads and say Amen. To act in this way would not result in unification.

However, if we were to summon a meeting of all the coworkers in order to discuss the need of Southeast Asia and then make an immediate decision regarding how to meet the need and whom and how many workers to send, this would be unification. Although there is indeed a great need in various places in Southeast Asia and a need for many to receive the Lord's commission, I have a solemn feeling that we should not take any action that might bring in the practice of unification. The most proper way to meet the need is for some of us to receive a burden from the Lord instead of having a unified move.

During the past few years, while traveling overseas, brothers have told me, "Brother Lee, you should send some saints to us from Taiwan." Every time I heard this kind of speaking, I inwardly felt uneasy and uncomfortable. This kind of speaking is not accurate according to the truth. First, why should I be the one who sends people? Second, why should people be sent from Taiwan? This kind of speaking carries the flavor of organizational unification, and it is wrong. Because there should be no unification among the churches, there should be no center.

Not Being Unified in Finance

The Lord has truly been merciful to us regarding the matter of finances, and by His mercy our finances are not organizationally unified. No one can tell us how much is received in offerings each month from all the churches. We also have no way to find out how much a particular brother receives. The general practice in Christianity is to unify and centralize the finances and then distribute them to others. Thus, people know exactly how much a certain mission or work receives each year. Although we may see a monthly financial report from a church, we have no way of knowing the amount enclosed in the envelopes that are designated for individuals and the amount given directly to the needy saints. This is proper. There is no unification or human control, and everything is under the authority of the Holy Spirit. This should be the principle of how we handle matters in the churches.

Not Having a Central Church or Person

Why should people be sent out from Taiwan? This concept

carries the flavor of unification. Why are people not sent to Taiwan from Hong Kong and other places? The brothers in Taipei should be able to write a letter to the brothers in Hong Kong, saying, "We need some of you to come here." We must not have the concept of a central church. Initially, we did not have this concept; however, it is possible that a kind of mixture has been brought into the church, that is, the concept that a certain local church is the center.

In principle, no local church is the center, and no person is the center. Our unique center is Christ our Head. All the churches should fellowship with and supply one another mutually, but we should guard against any suggestion that bears the flavor of unification. It is not fitting even to give people the impression that we might be unified. If any person or local church among us gives people the wrong impression, leading them to believe that he or the church where he meets is the center that controls everything, this is absolutely wrong. Everyone and every local church must be rescued from such an error.

The church does not have any center on the earth. If it had a center, it would be the heavenly Jerusalem (Heb. 12:22). On the earth the church does not have any center. Moreover, no man is the center of the church. If such a person rose up, God would surely remove him. This kind of thought, view, and concept must be eradicated completely from among us.

The church is different from a worldly organization. In worldly organizations there is unification. Each organization is three-dimensional, having different levels, some higher and some lower. However, the churches are completely flat, that is, on the same level. Every locality is on the same level, and every region is on the same level. The work in the Gentile region was not under the work in the Jewish region. Neither was Paul under Peter or Apollos under Paul. Although Peter was the leading apostle in the Jewish region, James took the lead in the church in Jerusalem. Although Paul was the leading apostle in the Gentile region, Apollos was not always under Paul.

On the one hand, there is order among the members of the Body. However, the order in the Body is limited to the members. There is no order among the churches. In this matter we have to be very careful. If we fall into unification, we will deviate. Once there is unification in regard to finance or the move in the work, the church has deviated. The natural man likes unification. When all the churches are unified and all have the same practices, it is easier to accomplish things. Nevertheless, this is not a proper condition. It is an erroneous condition.

The light in the Bible is very clear in regard to the administration of a local church being one. It is also very clear in regard to the work in a region being one, but there is no ground for a universal unification. For example, the administration of the local church in Taipei should be one. If it is not one, there will surely be chaos. It is the same in regard to the church in Tainan. Its administration should also be one. Moreover, if there is a group of co-workers serving the Lord together in a certain region, it is proper for the work in that region to be one. In other words, administrative oneness is permissible on a small scale but not on a large scale. There is absolutely no worldwide unification. We should never suppose that all the churches should practice the same things that the church in Taipei practices. If a brother who is an elder in the church in Taipei goes to Hualien, he should not assume that he will be an elder there. This is a wrong concept.

THE PROPER ATTITUDE

Not Being Individualistic or Loose

Strictly speaking, the church should not have a unification of administration and practice; however, it is dangerous to overemphasize this to the point that there is no oneness. Doing so gives people the opportunity to become proud and unruly and causes them to act recklessly. In order to maintain a universal unification, the Roman Catholic Church uses human hands to restrain man's unruliness. However, we do not desire to stretch out our hand. On our part, we would rather let unruliness run rampant than restrain it by human hands. Thus, there is a need that each of us would be on the alert to guard against and be watchful of the danger of unruliness. In other words, we need to be dealt with and to live in resurrection. We should not take the matter of not having an organizational unification as an excuse to say that we can act independently and recklessly. We should never be unruly and loose. Rather, we must turn to the Holy Spirit and learn to live in the Holy Spirit. In this way, each one of us will be led by the Holy Spirit. The result of being led by the Spirit is that we will have fellowship and will not act independently. In this way, our oneness will be the oneness of the Spirit, not the oneness of unification.

The way for the church to be built up is to be in resurrection. On the one hand, there should not be an outward unification among the churches; on the other hand, there is a danger of losing the oneness among the churches. This situation requires us to be delivered from the self and to live in the Holy Spirit and in resurrection. Some people may complain, saying, "This is so difficult. You say that we should not be unified and that we also should not act independently. Why do you make things difficult for us?" Awhile ago some young brothers came to me, asking, "Brother Lee, is it all right if we do something a certain way?" I said, "No." Then they asked, "What if we do it another way?" I still said, "No." Then they asked, "How shall we do it?" I said, "I will not tell you." Two days later they came and asked me again, "What do you think if we do it this way?" I said, "It is not good." Then they asked, "What if we do it another way?" I said, "It still is not good." Finally they asked, "Then what shall we do?" I told them, "I will not tell you." As a result, some were angry and said, "What is the matter with Brother Lee? He said no to whatever we proposed, yet he will not tell us what to do." This is the church. I should not tell you what to do; rather, you must prostrate yourself before the Lord and ask Him, "Lord, what should I do?"

Needing to Seek Confirmation

If a person comes to fellowship with me, saying, "Brother Lee, I have truly been dealt with by the Lord and have waited on Him for some time. As a result, I genuinely feel that this matter should be done in this way, but what do you think?" At this point, my spirit within will surely rise up and respond positively. If you have fellowship with the Lord first, and then seek confirmation, this is acceptable. This is genuine fellowship. You should not ask me to "unify" you. There is a great difference between these two ways of seeking fellowship.

Once some brothers from a certain local church came to ask me, "Brother Lee, what do you think we should do about a certain matter?" I answered, "I do not know. This is your business. Why do you ask me?" They thought that I was angry, but actually I said this so that they would realize that there are certain things that they do not need to ask me about. Apparently, it seems that I am a difficult person and that I always make things difficult for people. Actually, I make things difficult for people in order to impress them that anyone who participates in God's service should have neither the concept of unification nor the habit of being careless.

The reason I say that it is not right to do a certain thing one way or another way is so that you will learn to put yourself aside and live in the Spirit of resurrection. You must go to the Lord and say to Him, "O Lord, the meeting hall does not have the capacity to seat everyone. What shall we do?" Do not ask other people or other local churches. You yourselves must go to the Lord and ask Him. This does not mean that others do not have a concern for you or that other local churches do not care for you. What it does mean is that essentially this matter is between you and the Lord. Others' concern for you is another matter. These are two separate matters. Some young people have even asked me about the day of their marriage. They asked, "Brother Lee, on what day do you think we should get married?" Instead of asking me, they should ask the Lord. It is not acceptable to have unification, but it is proper to have spiritual fellowship in love.

In the church some unconsciously bring in errors because they are short of light or without light. Many times I am strict with the ones serving with me because I hope that among us none will bring in error due to a lack of light. Although the administration of a church is local, every saint in a local church should live directly before God. No elder should decide a matter for a saint. They should only bring the saints to the Lord. In the church life we often tend toward the extreme of acting individualistically and becoming loose and disorderly, or we go to the other extreme and bring in an atmosphere of unification. This is not only true in regard to one local church but in regard to all the local churches. Both extremes are wrong.

For example, in the matter of helping young people find a spouse, saints often hold an organizational concept and say, "We should not touch this matter. We must wait until the responsible brothers make a decision. Then everything will be all right." What kind of truth is this? The Bible never says that the saints cannot touch the matter of the young people's marriage and that only the elders can decide this matter. Perhaps some brothers will respond, "We did not intend to be this way." Yes, they may not have intended to be this way, but in their way of doing things, people can sense the flavor of organization.

Since there should be no organizational arrangement, some might say, "This is wonderful! Now it is all right for me to interfere in regard to others' marriage." If they do this, they will bring in confusion and the flesh. In all such matters, there should not be organizational arrangement, but there should be fellowship. There should be many older saints who love and fear the Lord and are concerned about the marriage of the young people. They can help introduce young people to one another. This is proper, and there is no need for the elders to exercise control in this matter. Nonetheless, this does not mean that the saints can act carelessly. Whoever has a desire to touch this matter should fear the Lord, learn to wait and pray in the Lord's presence, and seek others' fellowship.

We do not need unification, but we do need the oneness of fellowship. For example, when we have a feeling about something, we should go to the elders and fellowship with them. The elders will then fellowship with us concerning their feeling before the Lord. Thus, in such a way, inwardly we can become brighter, clearer, and more assured. This is real fellowship. Real fellowship is not to rule or to unify. This also applies to preaching the gospel. We should not say that if the elders have not decided that the church will preach the gospel, we should not have any gospel activity. This concept is wrong, and it limits the work of the Holy Spirit. If we have the feeling to preach the gospel, we should pray earnestly and look to the Lord to receive the burden. On the other hand, we need to also learn to fellowship with the responsible brothers. Both unification and independent action are wrong. The proper way is to learn to live before the Lord. Every one of us should give ground to the Head and allow the Holy Spirit the opportunity to work in us.

After we have received a burden from the Holy Spirit, we should fellowship with those who are experienced and who are in coordination with us. The responsible brothers should not have the attitude that if they have not made a decision concerning gospel preaching, the saints are not allowed to do it. This attitude is wrong. It is the error of unification, which should not be among us. Rather, the responsible brothers should have the attitude of looking to the Lord, praying to the Lord, and thanking the Lord for stirring up so many of the saints to have a burden for the gospel in the various districts. The responsible brothers should be spiritually observant so that whenever the saints receive this burden, they would fellowship with the saints, confirm the saints, bless the saints, and help the saints. The responsible brothers should never keep the church in their hands and turn the church into something unified. To do so is a serious degradation and error.

The church should not be in any person's hands. The church is in the hands of the Holy Spirit. I hope that all the saints would learn the lesson to withdraw their hand instead of stretching it out in the church. We must learn not to have confidence in ourselves, not to do things by ourselves, and not to walk according to ourselves but to fellowship with our companions in coordination and to fellowship with the leading brothers. We must learn to reject our independent activities, our moves according to human will, and our activities that are according to our insight and capability. Not only so, we must learn to place ourselves in the Lord's hand and fellowship with those in the church and with those with whom we serve. In this way we will receive help in the fellowship of the Body, from the Holy Spirit and from those who are ahead of us and more experienced than us. In other words, we must live in the Spirit of the Body and not live in our own feelings and flesh. We should keep this principle not only in one matter but in every matter.

CHAPTER TWO

SOME MATTERS RELATED TO FULL-TIME SERVICE

(1)

SERVING FULL TIME BEING A MATTER OF COMMISSION

Almost everything has its good points and its drawbacks. In the past few years, from 1952 until today, we have indeed had God's presence in the matter of serving full time. Many brothers and sisters have received the Lord's wondrous grace and brought great blessing to the church. However, there are several matters that we need to study carefully before the Lord. Some of these matters require that we be cautious, and others require that we make a few adjustments.

Everyone Needing to Serve

From the beginning, based on the light that God has given us, we have seen that every saved one, regardless of his occupation, should serve the Lord. Not only apostles, prophets, evangelists, and shepherds and teachers should serve God, but even a member who has a small gift should serve God. Those who serve in this way may not need to drop their jobs.

Serving God should be the primary concern, the basic work, of the believers. However, in order to make a living, the believers also need to hold jobs for their livelihood. Regardless of what kind of job a believer has, that job is only a side job. Even the sisters' managing and care of their homes are a side job. To us the most important matter on earth is to serve God. Hence, if the Lord's commission requires us to use all of our time to carry it out and if the environment allows our daily needs to be met, we should serve full time.

There are several ways for a full-time serving one's needs to be met. Some may have an amount of money provided by the Lord either through an inheritance or some other source. As a result, they have sufficient money to support their living. Some may be engaged in a business in which they do not need to work hard yet can still earn a living. Some may have their needs taken care of by the church or by individual saints who follow the Lord's leading. Some also have a strong faith in the Lord that enables them to get through. All of these ways allow the needs of the serving ones to be met. As a result, these saints are not only able to but should use all of their time to serve the Lord. Nevertheless, using one's time to serve the Lord is not exactly the same as being commissioned by the Lord for His work. In other words, everyone should serve the Lord, but how much time each one should dedicate to the Lord's service depends upon how much commission that person has received from the Lord and on the financial provision of their environment.

Even an apostle as great as Paul was forced to make tents (Acts 20:34; 18:3) due to environmental circumstances. The commission the Lord gave Paul required all of his time; however, the environment did not enable this. Consequently, Paul had no alternative but to set apart some time to make tents. If the environment had permitted him, he surely would have used all of his time to serve the Lord. Other people who serve the Lord may have a commission that requires only part of their time, not all of their time. Thus, they can also do something on the side.

We currently have almost one hundred brothers and sisters serving full time on the island of Taiwan. According to our observation, we feel that it is not suitable for some to continue serving in this way. This means that some of those serving full time should find a job. Not everyone who serves full time is necessarily called to do so, but every saved one should be a serving one. The amount of time with which a person should serve is based on the amount of grace he receives from the Lord and the provisions available in his environment. After observing the situation of the brothers and sisters who have been serving full time, we feel that some of them should take a job.

Initially, some began to serve full time because the Lord had arranged the environment, and they themselves sensed the Lord's commission. After two years, however, the Lord's arrangement in their environment may have changed. Consequently, they need to take a job in order to earn a living. This can be compared to the apostle Paul making tents. However, in this fellowship our focus is not on the environmental arrangements but on the serving ones' condition before the Lord and the commission that they have received from the Lord. The commission that some have received from the Lord is not sufficient for them to serve full time. Hence, they should take a job.

Serving Full Time Being Based on the Lord's Commission

Whether we serve full time is based not on how we feel but on the amount of work and the extent of the commission that the Lord has given us. All the brothers and sisters serving full time have a strong desire to do so, and they are willing to pay the price and give up their futures for the Lord's sake. There is absolutely no problem in regard to their heart; however, the Lord has not measured to some of them a sufficient amount of work or given them a commission that requires them to serve full time.

Some saints truly love the Lord, have been shown mercy by the Lord, have received the Lord's grace, and are weary of the world and the things of the world. They have a strong desire to come together with others every day to pray, to read the Bible, and to live before the Lord. This kind of desire is excellent, but it may not be the Lord's will, because there are many lessons that can be learned while working in a job. Hence, these saints need to work under others as nurses, teachers, and clerks. Although some saints can receive a high salary by working, they choose to not have a job because despite the difficulty in maintaining their living, they are content to serve full time. They feel that it is wonderful to not need to contact and strive with unbelievers. If they were to work as teachers, they would have to learn how to deal with the principal, the dean of academics, and other colleagues. For them, this is too troublesome. In addition, they would have to deal with many other matters in society that are bothersome. Instead of struggling and striving every day, they would rather contact the saints, preach the gospel, read the Bible, and pray. Actually, this lifestyle can be compared to entering a monastery. Without God's commission, they may merely become the same as nuns and monks.

In the Catholic Church many people enter monasteries for the same reason. They consider that the best human life is to be a monk or nun. By living such a life, they do not need to worry about their living, to struggle for worldly possessions, and to strive with those in the world. Instead, they need only to read the Bible in ease and comfort, living a "transcendent" life. From the standpoint of religion, this is quite good, and from the viewpoint of human philosophy, it is also not bad. However, spiritually such a life has little value. Ultimately, the question is not whether one way of life is better than another, but whether we are living according to the Lord's will for us and taking the way that the Lord desires us to take.

If the sisters like to stay at home and take care of the housework and serve their family, this is surely a proper human endeavor. However, some sisters feel that it is too troublesome to stay at home and do housework, serving their husband and children. They would rather serve the Lord full time. If this is the case, their serving is absolutely not according to the Lord's leading but an excuse for them to avoid human responsibility.

We may be able to conduct ourselves in a certain way, but we should not take our conduct as a teaching to speak to people or to instruct others. For instance, if a sister is single, she may tell others that it is best for females to remain single and that it is wrong for them not to remain single. We cannot criticize such a sister for being single. However, she should not take her condition of being single as a doctrine and instruct others to follow it. This is wrong. A sister should not serve full time in order to avoid the troubles of housework and of serving her husband and children at home. To serve full time in this way is comparable to living a life in a monastery. It is absolutely not according to the Lord's leading.

Serving full time is for only one kind of person, a person to whom God has given a work, a commission, that requires all of his time and who has an arrangement in his environment for his living. The basic condition is to have a commission. Consequently, some who are serving full time should not continue to serve full time because they have not been given much commission. Their heart toward the Lord is very good, their condition is also very proper, and there is no problem in regard to their person, but evidently, the commission they have received does not require all of their time. If such a person can hold a part-time job and serve part time, the benefits to both him and the church will be great.

NEEDING TO LEARN HOW TO DO THINGS

Everyone who serves the Lord has to learn how to do things earnestly. We must pay serious attention to this matter. Nothing wastes a person more than being a preacher. A young man who is a teacher is compelled by his job to excel at teaching. Methods of teaching are continuously improving, and ways to handle the students are also constantly being adjusted. These changes compel teachers to improve themselves. For example, if I were asked to be an elementary school teacher, I would probably not be qualified, because I have not kept up with the times. Everyone in an occupation knows that today's age is an age of competition. This competition forces everyone to learn and improve himself.

Suppose another brother and I were fellow teachers in a certain school. If thirty-eight out of his fifty students passed the examination to enter into high school, yet none of my sixty students passed the examination, surely the school would dismiss me, and no other school on the whole island of Taiwan would give me a letter of employment. Everyone is competing, and this competition forces people to learn how to conduct themselves and to do their work properly. Those who do not compete will not have a job. This is exactly the same in regard to salesmen. If one salesman sells $2,000 to $3,000 worth of merchandise a day, and another salesman sells $30,000 to $50,000 worth of the same merchandise a day, the manager or the head of the sales department will fire the first salesman or ask him to resign. At minimum, such a person will be forced to make improvements.

This is the same in regard to government employees. If two people are both secretaries, when the task that one secretary cannot handle is carried out immediately by a second secretary, the boss will give the second secretary important assignments and even a promotion. This is the actual situation in society. Competition forces people to advance. However, when believers become preachers, they become at ease and have no need to compete. They consider that whoever competes is fleshly. Consequently, this gives them the best excuse to be lax and negligent.

I recently observed the situation among us and discovered that many brothers and sisters' ability to handle matters is quite poor. This is because everyone is loose and wastes time. In the church there is no reward for doing things well, and there is no punishment for making mistakes. As a result, it seems that it is easier to become proud when things are done correctly and to make excuses when mistakes are made. This is not right. It is a huge mistake. Many reasons and excuses become shields for those who do not have a job and serve the Lord full time. Those serving the Lord do not want to be like Martha; rather, everyone wants to be like Mary. Instead of doing a lot of things, they would rather pray. What is this? This is the situation or condition of a monastery. Everyone likes to read the Bible and pray, but when matters come into their hands, they may create a big mess. This is truly improper. If those serving full time among us are loose in handling matters, in the future this will be a great loss to the church.

All those serving the Lord full time should learn how to handle matters in the church. Once we are short of aggressiveness or lack a sense of responsibility, we will not be efficient. Regardless of what profession a person is in, he cannot slack off. Once a person slacks off, efficiency is gone, and he will not obtain a good result. Most people do not slack off intentionally but are influenced by the trends around them. We have to admit that we are fallen and weak and cannot withstand the tests in the environment. We behave one way in one environment and another way in a different environment. If one is able to resist being influenced or subdued by the environment and instead subdues the environment, he is a most remarkable person. These people are far too few. Most people are controlled by their environment.

In the church the elderly brothers do not like to impose strict regulations on the full-time serving ones. The more the older saints have learned from the Lord, the more they dislike interacting with others as a superior ruling over a subordinate in the world, because such interactions are easily in the flesh. At the same time, the service in the church does not have an element of competition or of reward and punishment. Due to such an environment, the young full-time serving ones gradually enter into a state of ease and begin to slack off.

There are many things that I do not know, but there is one thing that I can boast of to the young people; that is, I know the proper way to do things. Since my childhood, I have daily had to deal with matters under the pressure of impoverished and difficult environments. Every day I struggled to handle different matters, and I learned to deal with every matter in a serious manner, not only in great matters but also in small matters. The pressure forced me to learn how to do things properly. For example, although others may have swept the floor thoroughly, when I sweep behind them, I am able to sweep up another pile of dirt. However, after I have swept the floor, others cannot find any more dust. This is competition.

Today many young people who serve the Lord in the churches are not like this. They do things in a rough and general way. Their heart is good and proper toward the Lord, but the environment they live in has caused their character to become loose. Looseness is a matter of habit and is developed unconsciously. The brothers who serve in the Taiwan Gospel Book Room are young, their minds are sharper than mine, and their education and literary talent may also be better than mine. Nevertheless, they can testify that in almost every matter, I have to go behind them and "sweep up" after them.

Whatever they do leaves a trail for me to clear away. Our attitude should be to do things so thoroughly that if the angels came behind us, they would have nothing to do. In this regard, the full-time serving ones among us have not made much improvement or advancement.

The way we work depends on how we handle matters, and the way we handle matters depends on the way we conduct ourselves. If we do not know how to conduct ourselves, we will not know how to handle matters, and if we do not know how to handle matters, we will not know how to work. These three things are closely related and affect one another. Everyone who is useful in the Lord's hands knows how to work. He who knows how to work also knows how to handle matters. This is certain. Some people are loose, and although we cannot say that they are wild, they are lazy. When a matter falls into their hands, it is very hard to obtain a result. Almost every person who knows how to handle matters is a strict person, and he does not do things as he pleases. The work in the church has little effectiveness because the full-time serving ones do not do things properly; their work is full of flaws and is neither perfect nor solid. The lessons they have learned are not solid. This is due to the absence of pressure in their environment.

Before I began to serve full time, I worked as an accountant. Every month I had to submit a monthly statement that included a balance report, indicating the profit and loss and the assets and liabilities. This report had to be precise, not even a discrepancy of one cent could exist. If there was a slight mistake, even though it might be a small matter within the department, it would become a great matter, a huge problem, when it reached the bank. As a result, I do not know how many times I had to check the monthly statement to make sure that there was not even a slight mistake. In addition, I also had to submit the statement on time, because the manager had to take it to the bank. As my boss, he did not care whether I had enough time or not, because he had to face the bank. Moreover, he had his own pressure to bear. If I had not done my work well, I could have lost my job or received a reduction in my salary. However, if I did the work well, not only was my job secure, but my salary was increased, and I received a share in the bonus at the end of the year.

These lessons and abilities are completely missing among many of the full-time serving ones. They did not intend to be this way, but their environment caused them to turn out this way. Although they may promise to do something, they can sleep peacefully. They know that if they do a good job, they may not be commended and that if they do a poor job, they will surely be rebuked. If they are rebuked, they realize that they must learn the lesson of humility, saying that this is the discipline of the Holy Spirit. Then they know the matter will be over. If anyone tries to pressure them, they will say that such an action is of the flesh. Consequently, the leading brothers have not dared to pressure them, and they have not learned the proper lessons nor had a proper walk.

The environment of the full-time serving ones is not the same as that of the working saints. The working saints are pressured by the matters related to obtaining a livelihood, such as salary, benefits, position, reputation, and future. They must learn how to conduct themselves and how to do things well. However, those serving full time lack the pressure of such an environment. It seems that whatever they say or do is fine and that whatever they do not say or do is also fine. It does not matter whether they preach the word, visit the saints in a way that is profitable, or do things properly. Although they do not intend or have the slightest intention to be like this, the matter of serving full time has fallen into such a condition.

The brothers who are older and who have spiritual weight in the church do not want to and dare not pressure these full-time serving ones. They dare not pressure them for two reasons: they fear that they might end up in the flesh and overdo it, and they fear that they might hurt the feelings of others. Consequently, they have let the full-time serving ones grow and develop on their own in a loose manner. I am concerned for these serving ones that one day they will become useless materials not only in regard to the Lord's work but also in regard to a job in the world.

This is a hidden peril for every full-time serving one. If you serve the Lord full time, you must be faithful to yourself.

Even without the pressure from the environment, you should learn to force yourself and create for yourself some demands and pressure. Please allow me to say an honest word. All those whom I have contacted in Taipei in the workers' homes, the bookroom, or the business office have not committed great mistakes, but they are very loose. If this continues, in the long run the serving ones will surely not have much future and usefulness. I know what I am saying. If some of them were to go into business, they would not make any money, and if they were to serve in the military, they would not win a war.

I do not desire to give those of you who serve full time a difficult time. I treasure your consecration. Every time I consider before the Lord how you have given your precious futures into the Lord's hand, I am almost in tears. Nevertheless, I have to tell you that you are too loose. Your looseness not only ruins yourselves but also causes you to fall short in your consecration. If you continue to be loose, in the long run your desire to be useful to the Lord will never be accomplished. You desire to be for the Lord, but your looseness will make you useless in His hands. If you continue to be loose, you will definitely become useless to Him, not to mention in other matters as well.

If you work in secular society, no matter what profession you are in, the environment will never allow you to be loose. Whether you are scholars, farmers, laborers, or merchants, once you enter into a certain field, the environment will force you to accomplish something. If you are a chef, you will need to cook gourmet dishes. Competition is everywhere in every profession. Even chauffeurs must compete. What causes full-time serving ones to be so loose is that in the Lord's service there is no salary or position, and no one seems to care whether or not you do well. Outwardly speaking, to serve full time is most noble. It also helps preserve a person's morality. However, it is also a risky matter. It is easy for those who serve full time to become loose in character and inefficient in handling matters, because they face no competition, do not need to worry about the future, and undergo no examinations or evaluations. Every serving one is free to grow and develop on his own and according to his conscience.

If the full-time serving ones do not have a serious attitude, they will become very loose. All men are fallen. If a person is loose for two or three years, he is through. This is especially true of the young people. Once they become accustomed to being loose, it is a real problem. This is my greatest concern and worry in regard to the young full-time serving ones. Unless we deal with this looseness and gird ourselves up, those serving full time will not be of much use in their future service. This is an extremely serious matter. It is said that if a man has been a preacher for four years, he is good for nothing else. Whether or not this word is too much depends upon how we conduct ourselves.

Young co-workers, you should not wait for others to gird you up. You have to gird yourself up. When a matter is committed into your hand, you must learn to do it thoroughly and solidly. You need to learn to gird yourself up. You should not be loose in what you do, and you should not overstep what you have been given to do. For example, if you live in the workers' home, you should not be loose in regard to how loud your voice is, because you are not the only person living there. Since there are many persons living in the workers' home, you should be strict even in the matter of your voice. This is not to be strict with others but with yourself. In every matter there are lessons to learn. The more lessons you learn, the more you will become sensitive to different situations. As soon as you encounter a situation, you will have a sense as to how to conduct yourself. The reason we are loose and insensitive is that we are not strict with ourselves.

Recently, the weather has become warmer, yet those serving full time still gave heavy blankets to the guests in the workers' home. The one in charge of the general affairs had no feeling about this. I do not believe that he did this to save money, because we are not short of money. Neither did he do this because he was not happy to receive guests, because we are all zealous to provide hospitality. Rather, he did this because of his looseness. His sensitivity to the needs of the service did not keep pace with the service. If we are providing hospitality, when we cover ourselves with a blanket at night, we should immediately consider what kind of blankets the guests are using.

In every matter someone should take responsibility, and he should be given clear instructions in regard to all the principles and details. Every matter should be done thoroughly, and everything should be well prepared. As soon as a person realizes that something is missing, he should replenish it immediately. Whenever something wears out, it should be fixed at once, and whatever is broken should be replaced immediately. In regard to the principles and details, we should provide clear instructions. For the past few days I have been very busy, yet it was I, not the one responsible, who first noticed and had a feeling regarding the heavy blankets. This may not be a big mistake, but neither is it the proper way to handle matters. If a person who does things in this way were to lead an army into battle, he would definitely lose the battle. If he were to invest in business, he would definitely lose money. Those serving full time must bear in mind that if their looseness remains unchanged, the work will have no future.

All those who know how to work are innovative. If there is nothing to do, they will find something to do. If there is something to do, they will do it in a thorough and solid way. However, among us the situation is exactly the opposite. Everyone is relaxed as if there were nothing to do. Even when there is something to do, it is not done thoroughly. If those serving full time do not change their character, we will have no hope for the future. May we all be girded up and learn to do things in a serious manner.

CHAPTER THREE

SOME MATTERS RELATED TO FULL-TIME SERVICE

(2)

GIVING ALL THE BROTHERS AND SISTERS AN OPPORTUNITY TO SERVE

We should not consider that the full-time serving ones are a special group of people. Moreover, we should not take the presence of the full-time serving ones as a reason to lessen the responsibility of or reduce the opportunity for other brothers and sisters to serve. Currently, there is such a trend in some local churches. Some saints have told the leading ones, "Since there are full-time serving ones, why do you want us to serve?" If the saints have such a concept, we should immediately reduce the number of full-time serving ones so that those who say such things will come and serve.

This kind of speaking has several possible implications. First, it indicates that the saints have the heart to serve but have not been given the opportunity. Second, it shows that although they desired to serve, they no longer have such a desire because they see that the full-timers are serving. Third, they may think that they are not needed because there are full-time serving ones. The thought behind the third implication is negative and unintentionally causes the full-time serving ones to become a special group within the church. Such a thought makes serving the Lord the business of the full-time serving ones and allows the saints who are not serving full time to rest. To counteract this, the responsible brothers in all the churches should endeavor and try their best to give the working saints opportunities to serve and be perfected. In this way, we can avoid the possibility of the full-time serving ones becoming a special class.

In every locality we should help the brothers and sisters see that serving the Lord is for everyone, regardless of whether they are serving full time or holding a job. It is an erroneous concept to think that only those who drop their jobs can minister the word in a ministry meeting. It is true that some—according to the Lord's leading, commission, and arrangement—drop their jobs to serve full time in the ministry of the word. This is good. However, it would be even better if some who hold jobs would also minister the word. Hence, we should not say that only those who drop their jobs can minister the word in a ministry meeting.

Likewise, some elders are very capable and have continued to hold their jobs. Others do not have the capacity to do both and have dropped their jobs in order to serve full time. There should not be the thought that only certain things can be done by full-time serving ones. In regard to serving in the church, no distinction should be made between those who serve full time and those who serve while holding a job. The only difference is how they maintain their livelihood. Some maintain a livelihood by holding a job to support themselves, others do so by looking to God for provision, and still others draw on their savings or inheritance. Thus, the difference is not in regard to how they function, or serve, but in regard to how they maintain their livelihood.

We should never regard the full-time serving ones as clergy. We should not even say that they are the "called ones." In the church everyone is a serving one. We simply have different ways of providing for our livelihood. The responsible brothers in all the churches need to make this matter clear to the saints. In the church there is no clergy; moreover, the full-time serving ones are not clergy. A capable co-worker may function much and yet continue to hold a job. Nevertheless, another co-worker, who has less capacity, may drop his job because he has received the Lord's commission and his daily necessities have been taken care of through an arrangement in the environment. This has nothing to do with either brother's competence in the service. The only difference between them is how they take care of their livelihood.

On my part, I do not know if one day the Lord will want me to take a job. However, if I take a job, it does not mean that I will stop serving the Lord. We should never think that if a person has a job, he does not need to serve anymore. Having a job or not having a job is not related to service but only to providing for one's living. In regard to serving the Lord we should not make a distinction between those who serve full time and those who hold a job. The full-time serving ones should not have the attitude that they need to do everything because they serve full time. Likewise, the working saints should not have the attitude that they do not need to do anything because others are serving full time. Both concepts are wrong.

Moreover, the full-timers should not be given special or favorable treatment in the church. It seems that in some of the churches the full-timers are given a special position; this is not right. They should not have any priority or special position in the church. In the church we may have different ways of taking care of our livelihood. Being a doctor, working as a clerk, and engaging in business are all for the purpose of providing a livelihood. Likewise, trusting in God's provision is also a means of caring for one's livelihood. Although there is a difference in the way saints earn a living, there is no difference between the saints in serving the Lord. In terms of service, all the saints should have an equal opportunity to serve. In this regard, we are all the same. All the brothers and sisters should be clear about this.

THE QUESTION OF FINANCIAL SUPPORT

I hope that all the churches will be more proper before the Lord in the matter of material offerings. Some of the churches in various localities have been doing well in this matter, and we thank God for this from the bottom of our heart. Some brothers and sisters have also been quite faithful toward the Lord in the matter of material offerings. Nevertheless, there has been a general weakness in this regard. I myself must bear the responsibility for this weakness. Since the beginning of the work in Taiwan, I have not helped the saints to learn to care for the workers.

The main reason for this is that I myself was not willing to do this, and when the responsible brothers desired to do it, I asked them not to. When we first came to Taiwan, it was extremely difficult to maintain a livelihood; thus, we were hesitant and unwilling to speak to the saints regarding taking care of the workers. Five years ago, on the whole island of Taiwan only four or five brothers had dropped their jobs to serve full time. In other words, there were only four or five people who needed financial support and help. However, these brothers were not able to receive support from the saints in Taiwan. I cannot blame others for this but only myself. In regard to this matter, I was inwardly conflicted. I felt that it is not proper for a worker to ask people for money. Moreover, I felt that I could speak freely concerning other matters, but I did not feel so free and at ease when touching the matter of money. Hence, I have not spoken clearly concerning this matter during the past few years. Now that seven years have passed without this matter being presented clearly, it has become a weakness in the churches. I hope that at present we could speak clearly regarding this subject so that all of us would have a thorough understanding of this matter.

In the very beginning we did not want to give the brothers the feeling that the workers were asking people for money. As a result, I never mentioned this matter. Because of this, a seed was planted that resulted in no one taking care of the living of the co-workers. According to my personal observation, the support for the full-time serving ones in the churches was very little. In fact, it was not sufficient even to cover their bus fares, let alone their daily necessities.

We know that the support for the full-time serving ones was very small. However, the offering for the expansion of the gospel was quite large. From this we saw that the saints were not necessarily limited in their ability to give material offerings. However, the regular offering for the needs of the serving ones was quite meager. Of course, there was a reason for this. The responsible brothers had fellowshipped with the saints regarding the needs related to the gospel; hence, the brothers and sisters spontaneously had a feeling and burden to give. Yet because no clear fellowship was given concerning the need of those serving full time, no one paid attention to or received a burden to give.

Based on my observation, if the Lord had not opened the support from other places, these full-time serving ones would not have had enough even for their bus fares. In the book of Esther, Mordecai told Esther, "If you remain silent at this time, relief and deliverance for the Jews will arise from some other place" (4:14). If we do not make a turn now and begin to take care of the full time serving ones, God will find help from some other place. It is truly a weakness if this matter is not carried out in a proper way. There are fifty saints serving full time in Taipei, but the support that the church receives is not enough to cover the living expenses of even five of them. The church in Taipei is the largest local church on the island of Taiwan, but the financial support provided for the co-workers by the saints who meet regularly and give according to the inner leading is not sufficient for five workers. In other words, ninety percent of the living expenses of the co-workers is not supplied by Taipei. This is an abnormal situation and a great weakness.

The lack of support does not mean that the saints are unwilling or unable to give. It simply means that there is a lack of awareness. Indeed, I am responsible for this lack. Hence, I not only have the burden, but I have the responsibility to speak to you regarding this matter. I hope that all the churches and all the responsible brothers will become clear before the Lord concerning this matter so that this weakness will not continue.

Regarding serving full time, although not every saint agrees, the majority of the saints realize that the churches are being supplied by the full-time serving ones. Today I must say a frank word: Since we all love the Lord and serve the Lord together, and we agree that serving full time is the proper way to render much supply to the churches, we should not put aside or ignore the daily needs of the full-time serving ones. This should not be our typical situation.

Since we need the service of the full-time serving ones, we

should supply their needs. Some responsible brothers from a certain locality came to me and said, "We have considered the matter seriously and have come to the conclusion that the church in our locality can support only two brothers to serve the Lord full time." Although this word may not sound good, it is based on the real situation. We cannot expect people to serve if we do not take care of their living; this is unrighteous. First Corinthians 9:14 says, "The Lord directed those who announce the gospel to live from the gospel." Moreover, in the law of the Old Testament it is written, "You shall not muzzle an ox while it treads out grain" (Deut. 25:4).

When we see that the full-time serving ones are busy all day long taking care of church affairs, we should not merely thank the Lord and say that this is wonderful yet neglect their needs. If we do this, it will be as if their feet are constantly treading out the grain, yet their mouths are muzzled. This is unrighteous. The responsible brothers, the brothers who love the Lord, and even all the brothers and sisters in all the churches should bear the burden before the Lord to supply the daily needs of the full-time serving ones. Although the full-time serving ones could have a job and a good income, they have laid aside the opportunity to earn a big salary because of their love for the Lord and the church. Hence, when we reap the benefit of their service, we cannot merely appreciate it without taking care of their living in a practical way.

I beseech all the responsible brothers to fellowship with the brothers and sisters in their respective local churches concerning this matter. In the past, the reason for the weakness and shortage of speaking on my part was that I myself am a full-time serving one, and it was difficult for me to speak of financial support. In the same principle, most of the brothers and sisters who have been helping the churches, especially the leading responsible ones, are serving full time; hence, they also have faced the same difficulty. As a result, this matter was not mentioned in any church. Since the brothers and sisters have not received leading in this matter, they have not paid much attention to it.

Moreover, the brothers and sisters in the churches may also have the concept that behind the full-time serving ones there must be a certain person or organization specifically designated to take care of their daily necessities. This is absolutely wrong. Among us there is no organization of work, mission, or center that controls the financial aspect. We have none of that. Hence, I hope we are all clear that we have not paid enough attention to the support of the serving ones in the churches and that we need to adjust this.

Some in the local churches are very concerned about the marriage of the young full-time serving ones. When they see that these serving ones have reached a certain age, they wish to see them get married. This is proper. But I would like to ask, "Where will they live after they are married?" Recently some have commended a certain brother, saying, "He is a good brother, and the church has truly benefited from his service; therefore, we should care for him in the matter of marriage." It is true that we should care for him, but have we considered where he will live after he is married? Those who introduce him to a sister should consider this matter on his behalf. They should not merely praise him for the supply that he has rendered through his service to the church. They should also consider where the couple will live after they are married. All the brothers and sisters should consider where it would be appropriate for them to live. Due to a lack of knowledge regarding this kind of service in the past, many brothers and sisters were not able to get married for a long time. We must learn to pick up this matter as a burden and lead the saints in the church to take care of this matter. Otherwise, the way ahead for those serving the Lord will be difficult.

In the beginning, when we were in mainland China, the matter of supporting the full-time serving ones was extremely difficult. Among the co-workers, none of our children have been willing to take this way. This is heartbreaking. For the past twenty years none of our children have been willing to take this way, because they know the kind of life that we live. Thus, even if we were able to change the heart of the entire earth, we would not be able to change our children's heart. Why do you think that none of the co-workers' children want to take this way? God in heaven is our true witness. This is heartrending. It is not that we have not prayed for our children. Every day we ask the Lord to remember them. However, living is a practical matter. From the day our children began to remember things, they have experienced how we live, and this has caused their heart to be hardened. Whose responsibility is this? I pray for the Lord's mercy that the eyes of the church may be opened and that the saints may see the real situation and not allow such a heartbreaking situation to occur again. In the church it should not be that one generation serves the Lord, but the second is unwilling to serve.

The Lord's work has been carried out here for approximately five years. Without the support of the heavenly grace, I am afraid that all the full-time serving ones would have become discouraged to the uttermost. I do not want to speak on my behalf, but I must speak on behalf of the young full-time serving ones and the Lord's church so that the church would be strengthened in this matter. Otherwise, if the current situation continues, the next generation will not follow in the steps of the preceding generations.

I hope that the brothers and sisters will receive this burden and present this burden to all the churches. We need to understand the aching feeling within the full-time serving ones and try our best to care for them. Throughout the years, there has been no organization of the work among us; there has been only the commission received through the ministry. We worship the Lord, because all the care comes from Him.

In 1948 a similar meeting to this one was held in Shanghai. In that meeting Brother Nee, an elderly sister, and I stood up and spoke a few words. In the end almost the entire audience wept. They wept because of their realization of the hardships experienced by those serving full time. Our hope is that the churches and the saints would learn to receive this commission before the Lord. In particular, the serving brothers who have a job should bear more responsibility in seeking an opportunity to speak to the brothers and sisters clearly regarding this matter. In this way the saints will come to understand this matter. It is difficult for the full-time servings ones to speak concerning this matter, but it is possible for the saints who have jobs to do so.

When you speak, you should not speak in a light way but

in a weighty manner. Moreover, you should not give people the impression that you are collecting donations; rather, you should cause the saints to feel that this is their responsibility in the service of the church. In this way God's work will be carried out. The sisters may not be able to bear the burden in the meetings, but they can enter into the Lord's presence and pray for the daily necessities of the full-time serving ones. We must try our best to help the saints realize that this is the greatest need in the church.

May the Lord, through our fellowship, cause all the saints to understand the difficulties that the full-time serving ones face, to bear the responsibility to care for these ones, and to share their blessing.

CHAPTER FOUR

SOME MATTERS RELATED TO FULL-TIME SERVICE

(3)

CHARACTER AND DISPOSITION

In principle, a person's character determines whether he will be successful and effective in his work or activities. This means that whatever a person does cannot escape the influence of his character. The character of a person determines how he conducts himself and how he works. Many of the problems among those serving the Lord are due to their character. Some men have spiritual problems and some have psychological problems. However, the most difficult problems are related to a person's character. Hence, as we learn to serve the Lord, we need to have much fellowship with the Lord and look to Him for His mercy and grace. Consequently, we must deal strictly with our character.

If we ourselves do not bear responsibility for dealing with the problems of our character, it will be hard for the Holy Spirit to do anything in us. The way we conduct ourselves and the way we do things are related to our character. We cannot say that the Holy Spirit never interferes and intervenes, but if we expect the Holy Spirit to build up a good character within us, we are seriously mistaken. The Holy Spirit does not do this kind of thing. Even if the Holy Spirit were to do such a thing, He would still require our cooperation, and we would still have to bear a considerable amount of responsibility. A brother's problems often lie in his character. When something is placed in some brothers' hands, it is ruined. Whatever they do is neither thorough nor solid. It seems that no matter what they do, they always leave something for others to finish. This is a matter of character or, we can say, a matter of habit.

One who serves the Lord should also have an amiable disposition; that is, he should enjoy contacting people. Some people by nature like to contact people, but this is useless because it is natural and not of resurrection. Only what is in resurrection can be useful. In our service we must be dealt with by God to the extent that we enjoy contacting people. At a minimum, we must deal with ourselves and compel ourselves to contact people.

In this training there are several brothers from overseas; however, the young serving brothers from Taiwan have not contacted them on an individual basis. Although the young brothers share the same room with the brothers from overseas, eat with them, and live with them day after day, they have not fellowshipped with any of these brothers. The young brothers from Taiwan do not know the names of those from Hong Kong or how many have come from Indonesia. This is our situation, and it is a problem. It is not easy for us to contact people. It is as if there is a wall through which even the Holy Spirit cannot break.

It is incredible that so many young serving brothers take their meals in the same dining hall and receive the same training in the same classroom, yet have no fellowship with one another. These young brothers should realize that the brothers from overseas have come not only to hear some messages but to seek fellowship. Indeed, the young brothers among us have an obligation to have much fellowship with them. If these young brothers fulfill their obligation, the brothers from overseas will be able to testify that they received more help from their personal fellowship than from their classes.

If we would receive more breaking and learn to have a proper spiritual disposition, we will receive more grace. Among us, grace is not contagious enough and has not spread adequately because we are too isolated. Even when we contact one another, we do so selectively. We contact only those whom we like. How will we be able to do things if we continue to be

SOME MATTERS RELATED TO FULL-TIME SERVICE

this way? Our disposition makes it impossible for us to serve the Lord.

During the training at Kuling from 1948 to 1949, Brother Nee said that in order to be useful in the Lord's hand, one who serves the Lord must be interested in people. When such a person sees people, he likes to study and contact them. When he sees new ones in the meeting, he will contact them and speak with them. One who serves the Lord must have this kind of disposition; otherwise, his service will suffer a great loss.

For example, a new one came to our Lord's table meeting and brought his whole family, yet none of our brothers and sisters went to speak with this family after the meeting. This is our weakness. Every servant of the Lord must grasp the opportunity to contact people. We should come to the meetings early in order to contact people. It does not matter if we come only five or ten minutes early. We should also contact people when the meeting is over. If every one of us were to contact one person before and after each meeting, each of us would be able to contact two persons every meeting. In this way, if we attend three meetings per week, each one of us would be able to contact six people every week. Some may say that this is unnatural. However, if we have an amiable disposition, a disposition that likes to contact people, we would feel that this is both convenient and spontaneous.

No matter what kind of meeting we are in, we need to contact people after the meeting; moreover, we should not speak with them casually, but we should minister grace to them inwardly. We all should have such a disposition—one that desires to contact people and know their spiritual condition before the Lord. This does not take too much time. Five to ten minutes are sufficient. Some brothers or sisters may have to leave immediately after the meeting, but we can walk with them for a distance or see them off to the bus stop. While we walk with them, we can talk with them. It does not matter if all we say is, "Brother, how are you? Where do you live?" Do not underestimate the effect of such simple words. Sometimes a few simple words are able to give enormous comfort and encouragement to others. Most businessmen realize that business deals are not made in the office but on a tennis court or in a coffee shop. Hence, when we contact people, we should not be too formal.

Our contact with the Lord is one thing, and our contact with people is another. The former can never replace the latter. When the Lord Jesus was on the earth, He was engaged in contacting both God and man. We cannot find a single case in the Bible in which the Lord went somewhere but did not contact anyone. He contacted people everywhere He went. Sometimes, according to God's leading, He withdrew from a certain place to be alone and purposely did not contact people. Except on such occasions, He was always in contact with people no matter where He went. Moreover, His preaching was always flexible. He spoke certain words to certain people at certain times. His speaking was never monotonous, dull, or formal. He contacted people every time and in every place so that He could impart grace to them. No matter what kind of people they were, He was able to minister grace to them in a timely way.

When the Lord Jesus lived on the earth, He contacted both God and man. He was joined to God at all times and in all places, and He also contacted people at every time and in every place. If everyone among us, regardless of age, learns and exercises to contact people, the church will be greatly blessed. On the surface, contacting people seems to be a small thing, but we do not know how many will be brought in as a result.

Many times after the meeting, we see that the saints, regardless of age, simply get up and leave. We rarely see any two of them linger and share with one another concerning their enjoyment in the meeting or open to one another regarding their personal condition. This is a great weakness and lack among us. To "talk shop" means to speak regarding one's line of work. What is our line of work? We have abandoned our future, given up the world, and forsaken fame and reputation. We are serving the Lord with our time, effort, and energy, yet we do not speak or do things related to our line of work. Do we really mean it when we say that we are interested in people?

Please observe the saints who have a job. After they get off from work, they hurry home, eat something, tidy themselves up, and rush to the meeting. In contrast, the full-time serving ones come to the meetings in an unhurried manner and set their watches accurately so that they will arrive at the meeting exactly at the scheduled time, neither late nor early. Then, like Mary, they enjoy the Lord quietly in the meeting. After the meeting, in the same manner as the working saints, they simply get up and leave. The working saints do not care about others and neither do the full-time serving ones. I would like to ask: Is this to behave according to our line of work? If we were fishermen and we were unable to catch any fish, we might simply give up, but how can we be unmoved when some of the fish come to us voluntarily and jump into our boats?

When we see the elderly saints, we need to learn from them, and when we see the younger ones, we need to supply them. The meeting hall is our fishpond—those who attend are the fish, and we are the fishermen. Since fishing is our line of work, we should do the work of fishermen. We should not forget our line of work. It is sad to see that among so many full-time serving ones not many are practicing their "trade." In the church life all the brothers and sisters should learn to contact people. Our heart for the Lord is precious, but our character presents a great problem. This is the reason that our meetings are low and our church life is dead and dull. We can no longer let ourselves be loose. We must gird ourselves up. May the Lord have mercy on us.

Chapter Five

KNOWING THE SPIRITUAL ASPECT OF THE CHURCH

(1)

THE CHURCH BEING IN RESURRECTION

If we have seen the types and the plan concerning the church, we will have a clear understanding of the church. In its spiritual aspect the church is an entity in resurrection. Doctrinally, we know this, but experientially, we may not have arrived at this stage. The church has two natures; it is the mingling of God with man and man with God. In other words, the church is the joining of God to man and man to God. This joining takes place in resurrection.

The Lord was incarnated to bring God into man, but this was only half of the journey. After the Lord was resurrected, He brought man into God. This completed the journey. Therefore, resurrection involved incarnation, but incarnation did not involve resurrection. Incarnation was not the whole process. Resurrection completed the process. In principle, when God is joined to us, it is incarnation, but when we are joined to God, it is resurrection. Resurrection is to bring man into God, that is, for man to be mingled with God. It includes both God being joined to man and man being joined to God. The church can exist only in resurrection. The church is produced by the joining of God with man and man with God.

We should not consider that what took place at Bethlehem was merely the Lord being born to be among men. We need to see that the intrinsic significance of what took place at Bethlehem is that God was brought into man and mingled Himself with man. The importance of what took place at Bethlehem is not merely a birth but that God was mingled with man. In general, Christians consider that what took place at Bethlehem was simply a birth, but we should see that it was a mingling. The significance of the birth is relatively minor, but the significance of the mingling is very great. Similarly, we should not consider the meaning of resurrection to be merely that Jesus was raised from the dead; rather, we need to see that resurrection was a mingling. The mingling that took place at Bethlehem and the mingling that took place in resurrection produced the church, a divine-human entity. The church is an entity in resurrection. This is not merely a doctrine but an experience.

The Experience of Resurrection

Experientially, what is resurrection? Anything that is of resurrection has passed through death, and anything that has not passed through death is not of resurrection. Of course, not everything that dies is resurrected, but everything that is of resurrection has passed through death. Furthermore, anything that is of resurrection is not the first but the second (1 Cor. 15:47). When we speak of the experience of resurrection, we need to ask ourselves whether our working and doing are of the first or of the second? Are they what we possessed originally, or have they passed through rejection? Do they have their original appearance, or have they been under pressure? Have they always been highly esteemed, or have they been put aside? Have they always existed, or have they passed through death? Likewise, when we examine ourselves in this way, we will begin to see how many things in us are natural and how many things in us are of resurrection. Anything that is spiritual and of resurrection does not stir up much feeling within us. In contrast, anything that is natural causes us to argue with others and stirs up much feeling. Hence, anything that is natural can easily stir up our feelings and cause us to argue with others. If we do not have any feeling, we spontaneously will not argue. A bench never argues, because it does not have any feeling.

In some local churches there are good brothers who serve together, but they often have arguments and different opinions.

This shows that they have not passed through death and resurrection. Whoever is in resurrection does not argue or have opinions. We must learn to deny ourselves. Not only should we deny our natural capabilities, but we should also deny our so-called spiritual views and spiritual gifts. If we deny ourselves constantly, we will genuinely experience resurrection. We should not think that if we deny our spiritual gifts and spiritual views, they will all be terminated and finished. We must learn that resurrection follows denial. Anything that is terminated after being denied is not of resurrection; that is, anything that cannot be raised up after being put to death is not of resurrection. However, resurrection fears neither death nor rejection. "Unless the grain of wheat falls into the ground and dies, it abides alone; but if it dies, it bears much fruit" (John 12:24). If our gift and insight are spiritual, we will not be afraid of rejection. The more we reject them, the more they will be resurrected.

In the natural realm we obtain things by striving for them. In resurrection we obtain things by rejecting them. Some people think that if they do not speak and exercise their spiritual gift, they will lose the opportunity. However, this concept is not according to resurrection but of the natural realm. In resurrection to die is to live, and to reject is to gain. We should give all the opportunities to others and put ourselves in the place of being nothing. In this way, many things of resurrection will be expressed through us. This is not a doctrine. This is altogether a matter of experience. In resurrection there is no feeling, and even if we have some feeling, we have to put it to death.

A person who is in resurrection does not fight, because he knows that his gain comes from his loss, that is, he gains by losing. He gains life through death. Unless the grain of wheat falls into the ground and dies, it abides alone. However, anything that is put aside and put to death will multiply at least thirtyfold, if not one hundredfold.

Previously, we have said that we need to be strict and diligent in doing things, but now it seems that we are saying that we should not strive in doing anything. In fact, these are two sides of one matter. Although there are two sides, the two sides do not contradict one another. In order to be strict, we need to pass through death. In order to endeavor the most, we need to stop. In order to be the most diligent, we need to halt. To stop and to halt are different from being loose. Many times we cannot stop ourselves, but God's hand stops us. When God's hand puts us to death, we may think that we are finished. Actually, it is at this moment that we enter into resurrection. Being loose is not equal to being terminated or put to death. A loose person can never enter into resurrection. Only a person who is strict with himself every day can enter into resurrection. A loose person can never achieve anything. Only one who is serious and diligent before the Lord can be brought by God's hand to the point where he expresses resurrection.

When we experience living in resurrection, the church will be realized among us. To be the church is not a matter of being meek, loving one another, or being humble. It is true that meekness, love, and humility can be found in the church. The saints surely love one another and are humble and meek toward one another. However, we should not consider that having these conditions is equivalent to having the church. The church is something in resurrection. Only when a person is in resurrection is he a "church-man." Human love is natural. People may love each other today and fight against each other tomorrow. Likewise, human meekness is natural. People may be meek today and argue with one another tomorrow. If a person has not passed through death, he will still have feelings that do not pertain to the church. For a person to feel that he loves people and is meek indicates that his feelings are not related to the church. They simply reflect his own naturalness.

The church is in resurrection; hence, whoever is in resurrection does not hold to his own feelings or argue with others. A person in resurrection may be very meek, but he has no feeling that he is meek. He may love people very much, but he has no feeling that he loves others. He may be very humble, but he has no feeling that he is humble. This is the proper condition of a genuine church. Throughout the churches we have observed many brothers who are good but who cannot work with others. They coordinate together, but often there are problems. Although this is common, it is definitely not a small matter. It is a serious problem for the brothers to not be in resurrection but to remain in their natural being. As a result of remaining in their natural being, they have opinions about others and are not able to be one with others. There are too many instances of brothers being in their natural man.

We all need to see the fact that the church is in resurrection. Anything that is originally ours is of the natural man. It is of the first man, and it is not the church. Anything that was there originally is in the natural man; it is not the mingling of God with man or the mingling of man with God. The basic principle in resurrection is the power of God's life operating in man, working in man, and bringing man into God so that all the fullness of God can be expressed through man. This expression is the joining of God to man and man to God. This is the Body of Christ, the church.

In the church as the Body of Christ a man's goodness and strong points have no place. In fact, every strong point and everything belonging to the goodness of man's natural being are problems to the church. For example, some are very diligent, but their diligence is inborn and natural. Hence, although the church may have benefited from their diligence yesterday, this benefit may eventually become a great problem to the church. In order for our diligence to be useful to the church, we must allow our natural diligence to be put to death by condemning it, rejecting it, and putting it aside.

Some may ask, "If we put aside our diligence, will we not become slothful?" If we become slothful once our diligence has been put aside, this shows that we certainly have no element of resurrection within us. If resurrection is in us, the more we put to death our diligence, the stronger and more multiplied it will become. In other words, once our natural diligence is put to death, a diligence in resurrection will be produced and multiplied. Only diligence in resurrection is profitable to the church and belongs to the church. The fact that the church is in resurrection is not merely a doctrine. May we be enlightened to see this.

The Way to Experience Resurrection

Much of what we are and have is still natural, and very little is in resurrection. This is because the shining in us is not sufficiently strong. In our practical experience we seldom condemn, reject, or put aside what is of us, that is, what we originally are and have by birth. For example, someone may tell us, "In your way of doing things, I have found much that is not appropriate and proper and that requires some adjustment." The way we react to this word is a test. Most people think that the proper reaction is to accept the critique and that to reject it is not proper. Actually, it is possible for either reaction to not be in resurrection. Resurrection is not a matter of accepting or rejecting the critique. When others point out our shortcomings, we may immediately have a certain feeling, but at the same moment, a light may shine on us, saying, "You need to put this feeling to death. This feeling needs to be condemned." Whether a person accepts or rejects criticism does not determine whether or not that person is in resurrection. A person may be quite able to accept another's criticism, but he may accept it by gritting his teeth. To accept it in this way is natural and is not of resurrection. The feeling must be put to death. Only then will his acceptance be in resurrection.

Similarly, being praised is also a test that manifests whether or not a person is in resurrection. If a person has the light of resurrection when others praise him, he will sense a hand within him pointing him to the cross. To some degree we have all had this kind of experience. From morning to evening, there is always a condemning hand within us, not condemning us in our conscience, but pointing at us and saying, "This is natural. This is in its original state. It has not been rejected. It is a grain of wheat that has not yet died." If this is our experience, we are in resurrection.

How much there is of the element of the church among us today depends upon how much we judge the natural things in us. When we are in one accord, we are not necessarily the church. Likewise, when we all love one another, we are not necessarily the church. For us to be the church depends upon whether or not we judge the natural things in us. Not only do the natural things need to be judged, but even the so-called spiritual gifts and spiritual views need to be judged. There should always be a finger within pointing at us and saying, "Is this spiritual insight the first or the second? Is this spiritual gift the first or the second? Is this Isaac according to birth, or is this Isaac who passed through the altar?" Although Isaac according to birth was good, he had to pass through the altar. By birth, he was not of resurrection.

Anything that has not passed through the altar is not of resurrection. Even if it is a gift obtained from God, it still needs to be rejected. Anything that is finished and gone after being rejected is not of resurrection. When something is of resurrection, the more it is rejected, the more it increases. Just one Isaac was put on the altar, but thousands of Isaac's descendants were gained. This is resurrection, and this is the church. Concerning this matter, we need to be enlightened and to receive grace. Once a person is enlightened, he will begin to sense something within him condemning him every day. It condemns not only the evil things but also the good things. It condemns not only the natural things but also the spiritual things. This condemnation is a seeing, a shining. It is the Lord's presence and His showing mercy to us. It is grace. It is God adding something additional to us.

When a person who has seen the principle of resurrection is criticized and senses that his feelings are stirred up, he will immediately sense something within pointing at him and saying, "You need to condemn this feeling. You need to reject this feeling." When others praise him and he senses a happy response, immediately something will convict him and say, "This feeling needs to be rejected." Likewise, when he relies on his gifts, something will also convict him, saying, "These gifts need to be put aside." When he is about to argue for the Lord's work, something will point at him and say, "This argument needs to be condemned." It is hard for us to say what this something is. Some say it is the condemnation of the cross. However, according to our experience, this condemnation is experienced by everyone who is in resurrection; hence, it is not related only to the cross. We do not have the boldness to say that this condemnation is related only to resurrection;

however, everyone who senses this kind of condemnation is in resurrection. It is in resurrection that the church, the coordination, the one accord, the expression of the Body, and every function of the Body are realized.

If the saints in the church are not in resurrection, their service and coordination will be only an exercise of tolerance, with each of us yielding a little to the other. Then when there are problems among us, a certain brother may mediate and remind us that for the sake of the Lord's name and work, we should forbear and be patient with one another. It is common to have this kind of mediation among us. For example, when two responsible brothers get into an argument, someone may rise up to mediate in this situation, saying, "Both of you are leading brothers, and if you argue like this, many brothers and sisters will be stumbled. Please calm down." This kind of mediation is not the church; rather, it is politics.

What is the church? The church is realized when brothers, while being judged inwardly, say, "O Lord, even if my proposal is of You, it still needs to be placed on the altar and rejected." This is the church. Whatever is in resurrection does not fear rejection. The Son of God fell into the ground and died to become many sons. The only begotten Son died, and many sons were produced. Whatever is of God does not need to be safeguarded by us. Some brother may ask, "What if we suffer loss? What if things are spoiled? What if things are delayed?" If we suffer loss, let us suffer loss. If things are spoiled, let them be spoiled. If things are delayed, let them be delayed. We must place everything in God's hand.

The crucial matter is whether we have passed through judgment and whether something within has inwardly convicted us. When there is nothing more to be said or done, when there is absolutely nothing more, then there is resurrection. If something can still come forth after everything is dead and finished, it is resurrection. In the church man's zeal and cleverness should be judged. Even our giving of a message should be judged. People are concerned that if they miss an opportunity, they may never have the opportunity again. To this, the Lord will say that it is not a matter of having an opportunity but a matter of whether it is of the first or the

KNOWING THE SPIRITUAL ASPECT OF THE CHURCH 157

second. God has allowed many, many opportunities to pass. He has been missing opportunities for the past six thousand years. Instead of paying attention to opportunity, God keeps asking whether it is of the first or the second, whether it is of man or of man in God. Is it man alone, or is it the mingling of man and God? This is what God cares for.

Everything that is merely of man is natural, but everything that is of the mingling of God and man is in resurrection. If a person has been shown mercy, inwardly there is always a finger pointing at him, just as when he was first saved and began to pursue the Lord. Within a newly saved one there is always a story of love. Although he cannot utter or explain it, this story is in him, and it causes him to desire and incline toward the Lord all the time. Even when he is doing a small thing, a feeling of love touches his inward being. In the same way, if he has been shown mercy, today there is another story in him, that is, a story of conviction, a story of being rebuked. Not only are bad things rebuked, but also good things are rebuked. Both good things and bad things are rebuked. What is of the self is rebuked, and even what is of God is rebuked. Natural things as well as spiritual things are rebuked. Everything that is done through a human hand is rebuked and condemned. Everything of Ishmael and Isaac must be put aside. The church is realized through this unceasing rebuke.

Due to a shortage of this experience among us, we cannot perceive much of the church. If man cannot enter into God and God cannot be expressed from within man, not much of the church will be expressed. The story of resurrection is that man enters into God and allows God to be continually expressed from within him. Only in resurrection can the church be realized. This is a crucial point. If we miss this point, everything is just doctrine.

THE CHURCH BEING SPIRITUAL

Resurrection and the Holy Spirit Being Inseparable

The church is spiritual. It is something entirely in the Spirit. Everyone who has experienced resurrection and the Holy Spirit knows that resurrection and the Holy Spirit cannot be separated. Doctrinally, resurrection is resurrection, and the Holy Spirit is the Holy Spirit; however, experientially, the two are one. To be in resurrection is to be in the Holy Spirit, and to be in the Holy Spirit is to be in resurrection. The Holy Spirit is resurrection. The two are one. John 7:39 says, "The Spirit was not yet, because Jesus had not yet been glorified." Jesus entered into His glory when He resurrected (Luke 24:26); hence, the Spirit was not yet, because Jesus had not yet resurrected.

In incarnation God became a man, the Lord Jesus, and in resurrection the Lord Jesus became a life-giving Spirit. This is what John 14 reveals. God became the Lord Jesus through incarnation. The Lord Jesus then became the Spirit through resurrection. Thus, the Spirit cannot be separated from resurrection. On the evening of the day of the Lord's resurrection, He came and stood in the midst of the disciples and breathed into them, saying, "Receive the Holy Spirit" (20:19, 22). The Spirit whom the disciples received was the Spirit anticipated in John 7:39. Thus, to be in resurrection is to be in the Holy Spirit; to say it in reverse, to be in the Holy Spirit is to be in resurrection.

The Church Existing Only in the Holy Spirit

If a brother's feelings are stirred up when he is criticized or praised, this indicates that his feelings are not in resurrection and not in the Holy Spirit. However, if he allows his feelings to be condemned, rejected, and judged, and they rise up again, they will be in resurrection and in the Holy Spirit. Therefore, in our experience resurrection and the Holy Spirit cannot be separated. To live in one's self is to live in the natural being. To live in the Holy Spirit is to live in resurrection. The two—the Holy Spirit and resurrection—are one.

When a brother is having problems, it is common to suggest that he be visited by a brother who has a friendly relationship with him. Is this suggestion from the Spirit or from the mind? Undoubtedly, it is from the mind. Moreover, is this suggestion of resurrection or is it natural? Surely, it is natural. If we have seen this principle, we will realize that our good intentions are outside of the Spirit. They are in our self and not in resurrection. In the church life people often suggest certain methods to help the brothers and sisters who live together pass through certain dealings so that they will become well behaved. Are these dealings in the Spirit or outside the Spirit? On the one hand, it is difficult for us to discern what is of the Spirit and what is natural, but on the other hand, deep within we are able to discern and know whether something is in our self or in the Spirit. It is marvelous that although it is not easy for us to distinguish what is of the Spirit and what is of the self, deep within we are able to know what is of the Spirit and what is of the self.

The church is entirely a matter of being in the Holy Spirit. The church is not a matter of being truthful or being false. No doubt, there is no falsehood in the church, but neither is the church a matter merely of truthfulness. The problem is that man pays more attention to such matters as good or evil and truthfulness or falsehood than to the Holy Spirit. As a result, there is not much manifestation of the reality of the church. According to God's design, all the fullness of the Godhead dwells in Christ bodily (Col. 2:9). Moreover, the Lord Jesus, including all that He is and has accomplished, has become the life-giving Spirit (1 Cor. 15:45b; 2 Cor. 3:17). Today the church is the enlargement of Christ. Apart from the Spirit, there is no Christ, and apart from the Spirit, there is no church. In other words, apart from the Spirit, the riches of Christ cannot be expressed among us. Man's positive attributes, goodness, and virtues are not the church. The church can be expressed only when we reject these things and live in the Holy Spirit.

CHAPTER SIX

KNOWING THE SPIRITUAL ASPECT OF THE CHURCH

(2)

THE CHURCH BEING HEAVENLY

The Church Being Heavenly according to Its Nature

The church is in resurrection, and it is spiritual and heavenly. Ephesians 1 and 2 clearly show that the church is seated together with Christ in the heavenlies (2:6) and that all the blessings that God has bestowed upon the church are spiritual blessings in the heavenlies (1:3). According to the position of the church and the blessings that the church has received, the church is truly in a heavenly realm. The heavenly nature of the church is one of the crucial blessings that the church has received. The nature of the church is heavenly.

If we carefully analyze Ephesians 1 and 2, we will see that these chapters speak of the position, nature, function, and sphere of the church. According to these two chapters, the church's position, nature, function, and sphere should be heavenly. *Sphere* refers to the church's expression, the condition that the church manifests. Every aspect of the church should be spiritual and heavenly, because the church is in resurrection.

In Ephesians 1 and 2 *heavenlies* indicates not only the heavenly place but also the heavenly nature of the church. The Greek word for *heavenlies* has various connotations. In English we can differentiate its meaning by also translating it as "in heaven" or "heavenly." Hence, *heavenlies* in Ephesians 2 includes place, yet its emphasis is on the heavenly nature, not the heavenly place. According to place, the church is still on earth and not in heaven, but according to its nature, the church has been brought into the heavenly realm through the resurrection of the Lord Jesus. Thus, the emphasis of *heavenlies* is on nature.

In the Bible resurrection is never separated from ascension. Resurrection and ascension are always related to one another. Especially in Acts, resurrection is altogether related to ascension. This can be compared to the palm and the back of the hand. They are always related and cannot be separated. A hand cannot have only a backside without a palm or a palm without a backside. Likewise, resurrection and ascension cannot be separated; they are joined to one another. The resurrection of the Lord Jesus brings man into God, that is, into the heavenly nature. In other words, the Lord Jesus' resurrection brought humanity, which He put on and was joined to, into the heavenly nature. Some have proposed that in Ephesians 2 the word *heavenlies* should be translated as "heavenly realm." It is somewhat misleading to use the word *realm*, because realm is a matter of sphere. The Lord brings us into the heavenly realm, which is not only a matter of sphere but also a matter of nature.

First Corinthians 15:47 says, "The first man is out of the earth, earthy; the second man is out of heaven." The first man is earthy, and the second man is heavenly. The first man is Adam, who was made from the dust of the earth. The second man is Christ. The second man spoken of in this verse is not the Christ in incarnation but the Christ who has passed through crucifixion and resurrection. Adam and his descendants are earthy, but Christ and the people whom He gained in resurrection are heavenly. Thus, according to 1 Corinthians 15, the natural man is earthy, but the regenerated man of the new creation in Christ is heavenly. How can we who were originally earthy become heavenly? The explanation lies in Christ's incarnation, death, and resurrection. Through Christ's incarnation, death, and resurrection, our earthy nature has been transformed and brought into the heavenly nature.

Heaven Being Related to the Authority of God

The Holy Spirit is resurrection, and God is resurrection.

Resurrection is God Himself, and God is the Holy Spirit; therefore, the Holy Spirit is resurrection. In the Bible heaven refers not only to a place but, even more, to something mysterious. If we read the Bible carefully, we will see that God and heaven cannot be separated. God and heaven are joined together.

Luke 15:18 says, "I have sinned against heaven and before you." This utterance is very particular. It shows that God and heaven are connected. We cannot say that God is heaven, but we can say that heaven is joined to God. God's nature is spiritual and heavenly. The Bible says explicitly that God is Spirit (John 4:24), but it does not say that God is heaven. In the light of the Bible, however, we can see that God's nature is not only spiritual but also heavenly.

What does *heavenly* mean? This is a very difficult question to answer. God is Spirit; hence, His nature is spiritual. The Bible also shows that anything that is of God is heavenly. In 1 Corinthians 15 the second man, Christ, is out of heaven (v. 47). The New Testament frequently mentions the heavens, and the Gospel of Matthew repeatedly makes mention of the kingdom of the heavens.

In the Old Testament, Daniel 4:25-26 speaks of the heavens' ruling. It seems that Daniel considers the heavens as something living. When he says that the heavens do rule, he means that God rules over men. However, verse 26 does not say that God rules but that the heavens rule. Thus, heaven has a very particular significance in the Bible. In the New Testament, Hebrews places great emphasis on heaven and the heavenly nature. It refers to our calling as "a heavenly calling" (3:1). Moreover, it also says that today Christ is "a great High Priest who has passed through the heavens" (4:14) and that the holy place into which He entered is in heaven itself (8:1-2; 9:24).

The Lord prayed in Matthew 6:10, "Your kingdom come; Your will be done, as in heaven, so also on earth." This kingdom is the kingdom, or ruling, of the heavens. Therefore, in this verse the emphasis of *heaven* is God's authority. Every heavenly matter is full of God's authority, God's lordship, and God's position. In contrast, whenever we speak of something spiritual, we emphasize God's nature and life more than His authority. The fact that a person is spiritual means that he is full of God's life inwardly. Although God's authority is realized through the Holy Spirit, the Bible says that the Holy Spirit is the Spirit of life (Rom. 8:2) and the Spirit of power (Luke 24:49). Moreover, it never uses the term *the Spirit of authority*. In the Bible the Holy Spirit is chiefly spoken of in regard to God's life, and in Romans 8:2 He is even called the Spirit of life. In contrast, in the Bible the term *heaven* is directly associated with the authority of God. Whenever heaven is spoken of in the Bible, the emphasis is God's authority. The most obvious examples are "the heavens do rule" in Daniel 4:26 and "the kingdom of the heavens" in Matthew (5:3, 10, 19-20).

The opposite of being heavenly is to be earthy. To be earthy means to be earthly and worldly. What does it mean to be worldly? To be worldly means to reject God's authority and ruling. To be heavenly means to submit to God's authority. Of course, to be heavenly also has many other connotations, but according to the Bible, to be heavenly primarily denotes being under God's authority. Every matter that is earthly is not in submission to God's authority, but every heavenly matter is in submission to God's authority. Hence, there is a big difference between being heavenly and being earthly. The difference lies in whether or not there is submission to God's authority. Earthly matters are not in submission to God's authority but heavenly matters are.

The garments that the children of Israel wore had fringes on their borders, and on each fringe was a cord of blue (Num. 15:38-40). This signifies that their conduct and behavior were restricted by heaven. To be restricted is a matter of authority. The cord of blue on the fringes of the borders of their garments restricted their steps. This signifies that their conduct and behavior before God were under the restriction of heaven. Garments signify man's conduct, and the blue cord on the fringe of the border of the garment signifies that a man's conduct is not only heavenly but also under the rule of heaven. If the blue cord signified merely being heavenly, it could have been placed on another part of the garment. There would have been no need to place it on the border of the garment. By being placed on the border of the garment, it encircled their footsteps. The encircling of the footsteps indicates authority, because encircling is a restriction. To be restricted is to be under authority.

To Be Heavenly Being to Submit to the Authority of God

The main significance of the church being heavenly is that it is under God's authority. The nature of the church is to submit to God's authority. Water is not viscous, but oil is. Hence, viscosity is the nature of oil. In the same way, heaven also has a nature. Its nature is to submit to God's authority. *Heaven,* as spoken of in the Bible, strongly implies submission to God's authority. To further illustrate the different natures of things, let us consider the difference between the pliable nature of a handkerchief and the rigid nature of a piece of chalk. If a person attempts to fold a piece of chalk, it will snap. This is because its nature cannot withstand folding. However, if a person folds a handkerchief, it will not snap like the chalk. This is because its nature can withstand folding. Hence, the difference in nature between a piece of chalk and a handkerchief is that one can be folded easily and the other cannot.

In order to submit to God's authority, His creatures must have the nature of heaven. They must be heavenly. In the universe only the heavens submit to God's authority. The particular nature of heaven is that it submits to God's authority. Wherever heaven is, God's authority is there. Hence, to be heavenly is to have the nature of submitting to God's authority.

Apart from the Spirit of God, we cannot touch the life of God. God's life is in the Spirit. If we want to touch God's life, we must touch the Spirit of God. Hence, the Spirit of God is God's life. In the same principle, God's authority is in heaven. Thus, heaven represents God's authority. The prodigal son in Luke 15:18 said, "Father, I have sinned against heaven and before you." This implies that when a sinner commits sins, he sins against heaven; that is, he sins before God the Father who is in heaven. When a sinner sins, he offends God and violates

God's authority. Since God's authority is in heaven, whenever a sinner touches God's authority, he touches heaven. God's ruling is heaven's ruling.

The primary significance of the church's being heavenly is that the church is under God's authority. The nature of the church involves submission to God's authority. According to its nature, a handkerchief is pliable because it is soft. If a handkerchief is not pliable, something is wrong with it. Likewise, according to its nature, the church submits to God's authority. Thus, it is not difficult for the church to submit to God's authority. If the church does not submit to God's authority, something must be wrong with the church. The church's submission to God's authority is due to her heavenly nature.

Most people understand heaven as a blessing. Many Christians think that once they "go to heaven," they will enjoy peace and blessings. They even sing about it. This thought is entirely from the Roman Catholic Church. Their basis is Revelation 7. However, Revelation 21:2 says that the New Jerusalem will come down out of heaven from God. People think that they will to go to heaven, but the Bible tells us that the New Jerusalem will come down out of heaven. Not only will men not go to heaven, but heaven will come down to the earth. Man pays much attention to going to heaven, but God pays attention to the earth. Some men dream all day long about going to heaven, but God is concerned only with coming down to the earth.

The source of the concept of the blessing and happiness of heaven is entirely something of the Roman Catholic Church. The Roman Catholic Church uses the superstition of the blessing of heaven to distract people. Many teachings in Chinese Buddhism and Taoism are similar to this. However, we who believe in the Lord must see that in the Bible heaven is a matter of authority.

There is a difference between being heavenly and being earthy. They are altogether two different natures. One is glorious, and the other is lowly. One is of God, and the other is not of God. Although everything that is with God and is heavenly is blessed, joyous, peaceful, and bright, the emphasis in the Bible is that heaven is the place entrusted with God's authority. To nullify heaven is to nullify God's authority. Therefore, the Bible says that the heavens do rule (Dan. 4:26). The ultimate dwelling place of God is the earth. The New Jerusalem will come down out of heaven. Hence, heaven is a place not for enjoying blessing but for ruling.

Since heaven is related to God's authority, Satan also attempts to usurp it. Ephesians 6:12 speaks of the spiritual forces of evil in the heavenlies. This shows that Satan is the ruler of the authority of the air (2:2) who rebels against God and attempts to encroach upon God's authority. God's enemy encroaches in the sphere of God's authority in the air; thus, spiritual warfare is a matter of being heavenly and having authority. It is not a matter of blessing. For the church to be heavenly means that it is under God's authority. Only when the church is under God's authority can it deal with the enemy who encroaches upon God's authority. This is altogether not a matter of blessing but a matter of warfare, and it is not a matter of peace or joy but a matter of authority.

Some may say, "Does not Ephesians 1:3 speak of the blessings in the heavenlies?" If we read the context carefully, we will realize that these blessings are not peace or joy but the Father's choosing, the Son's redemption, and the Spirit's sealing. Certainly, all these items are heavenly, but we should not forget that heaven takes God's authority as its center. The primary significance of heaven is God's authority.

The Heavenly Condition of the Church

The church is heavenly not because it does not have a board of directors, does not elect elders by voting, and does not collect donations. Neither is it heavenly because it has a group of elders who have been appointed by apostles and who manage church affairs nor because it puts out an offering box during the meeting for the saints to give willingly. The church is heavenly because it is under God's authority. Why do people want to vote for and elect elders? It is because there is no authority of God. Why are there boards of directors? It is because such boards are related to human ruling. Why are there worldly methods? It is because the methods of the world are related to human ruling. The more we submit to God's authority, the fresher and brighter the heavenly "color" in us will become. Philippians 3:20 says, "Our commonwealth exists in the heavens." This means that we are heavenly citizens who submit to God's authority. To be a heavenly citizen is a matter of authority. Only those who submit to God's authority are heavenly.

This shows that the significance of being heavenly is that a person submits to God's authority. To be heavenly is to allow heaven to rule in us and to let God establish His throne in us. Methods cannot make us heavenly. We are heavenly only by submitting to God's authority. If we are different from others merely as the result of certain methods, we are still of the world. For example, in the Lord's Day meeting many Christian groups pass a collection plate in order to receive donations; however, on our part, we put out an offering box and leave it to the brothers and sisters to offer willingly. This difference is only a matter of method, and neither method makes the church heavenly. Whether or not the church is heavenly in regard to the giving of material offerings is determined by whether or not God's authority rules in this matter. The denominations elect elders by voting, whereas among us, apostles appoint elders. Nevertheless, this difference is a matter only of method; it does not cause us to be more heavenly than the denominations. No method is able to make us heavenly.

If the difference is a matter only of method, then the election of elders is just as earthly as the apostles' appointment of elders. The question is not a matter of method but of God's authority. Only God's authority makes us heavenly. The reason we do not have elections is that elections do not allow God to freely exercise His authority. However, if the apostles do not allow God to freely exercise His authority in the appointment of elders, we should reject such a method. To appoint elders in this way is not heavenly but earthly. Only when God is allowed to have the authority will the church be heavenly. This is the same in regard to preaching the word. We are heavenly only when we allow God's authority to be exercised. In some places, the ones who minister the word take turns speaking. This week Brother Chang will speak, next week Brother Lee will speak, and the following week Brother Wang will speak. Taking turns is altogether a worldly method, and we should reject it. To preach the word, a person must be willing to submit to God's authority and allow God's authority to have a free way. Only this kind of preaching is heavenly.

It is not methods that make us heavenly; rather, it is God's authority. The most important matter for maintaining the heavenly nature of the church is that the church stays under God's authority. This means that in every matter in the church there is God's throne, or God's authority. Whether or not a church is heavenly is determined not by whether things are done one way or another or by whether they are done in a way that is scriptural or unscriptural but by whether they are carried out in submission to God's authority. We must continually learn the lesson of submitting to God's authority. This is altogether not a matter of doctrine or of the interpretation of the Bible. On our part, we do not elect elders, because electing elders is not according to the Bible; rather, in accordance with the Bible, the apostles appoint the elders among us. Likewise, those ministering the word among us do not take turns in preaching the word, because there is no such practice in the Bible. However, although we are scriptural, being scriptural does not necessarily mean that we are heavenly. Only when we allow God to rule are we heavenly. This is true in the appointing of elders, in the preaching of the word, and in the managing of finances. We must always ask whether God's authority is being carried out in this matter. This is the question of questions, the unique question.

All earthy people are rebellious toward God. Everything earthy is the serpent's food, that is, something for Satan to devour. However, now there is salvation; that is, heaven has come to earth through the Lord's incarnation. Moreover, in His resurrection the Lord has brought people from the earth to the heavens. He has caused those who would not and could not submit to God's authority to be willing and able to submit to God's authority. When the Lord was resurrected, He brought His redeemed ones to the heavenlies. The emphasis of His bringing them to the heavenlies is not related to place but to nature. The church, in her nature, is altogether submissive to God's authority.

The church being heavenly is not a matter of method or outward appearance but a matter of having authority inwardly. Are matters among us in the hands of man or in the hands of God? Is man ruling, or is God ruling? This determines whether or not we are heavenly. If we do everything according to the Bible yet do not have God's authority, we are not heavenly. To be heavenly means that God's throne is present and that the heavens are ruling. To be heavenly is to cast out God's enemy and to deal with Satan who is in rebellion against God's authority. To be heavenly is to put the enemy to shame under God's authority. To be heavenly means that although God's enemy rebelled against God's authority, the saved ones submit to God's authority. To be heavenly is not a matter of being blessed or of being in a certain situation or condition; rather, it is a matter of nature. For example, the nature of glass is that it is brittle and breaks if it drops to the ground. In contrast, the nature of rubber is soft; thus, no matter how it is dropped, it will not break. Similarly, the church has its particular nature, that is, a nature that submits to God's authority. Today, apart from the church, no one submits or is even able to submit to God's authority. However, because the church is heavenly, it is able and does submit to God's authority.

Since the church is heavenly, whenever we depart from God's authority and do not submit to God's authority, we lose the nature of the church. The church is of resurrection and is spiritual and heavenly. In the church there is nothing that cannot and does not submit to God's authority. The entire church can and does submit to God's authority because it is in its nature. Through resurrection Christ brought the church into such a nature. Christ has a nature that submits to God's authority, and the church also has this nature. The reason that the church is able to rule is that it is heavenly. The reason that the church can bind whatever has been bound in the heavens and loose whatever has been loosed in the heavens is that the church is heavenly (Matt. 16:19). The reason the church is able to represent God to rule over everything on the earth is that the church is heavenly. As soon as the church loses its heavenly nature, it immediately falls under the authority of the world. Hence, the church must be heavenly.

Chapter Seven

RECEIVING PEOPLE IN THE CHURCHES

AN EXPLANATION OF THE FACT AND THE PRINCIPLE

We now come to the question concerning our receiving of people in the churches, that is, how to determine whether to baptize someone. To baptize someone is to receive him. This matter is clear to us in principle, but we still need to carefully consider its practical aspect. For the past few years our principle for receiving people, that is, for determining whether or not to baptize people, was right. However, we must confess that we have been weak and short in carrying out this matter. We may not have been clear at the time, but looking back, the facts indicate that our practice had certain defects. For example, some who did not have a relationship with the Lord were baptized.

We were clear concerning the principle that only a saved person should be baptized, that is, a person who has believed, who has been saved. We should not baptize those who receive the Lord Jesus nominally but do not receive God's life and have no inward relationship with the Lord. In our practice, however, we have baptized some who we thought were saved but who did not actually have a relationship with the Lord or have God's life within them. In some localities we have met people like this. Consequently, we should reconsider our practice. Although our principle is right, the dependability of our practice is questionable.

In the past, at certain times, we baptized many people; however, few among them remained after being baptized. One reason is that we were not able to take care of such large numbers adequately. Although they were truly saved, they eventually became cold due to their environment or inadequate care. Some may have remained cold for two years but turned and were revived during the third year. Nevertheless, we cannot deny that some, perhaps a small number, were never clear concerning salvation, yet due to our inaccurate judgment, we baptized them. In the end, they left after being baptized.

We can point to several people whose salvation we initially doubted and who, we are now quite certain, were never saved. Despite our initial doubts, we indeed baptized them. Now they neither meet nor bear the testimony of being Christians. This compels us to reconsider our practice.

We must admit that we have viewed the matter of receiving and baptizing people too lightly and inadequately, without realizing its seriousness. This is especially true of the brothers who contact people and are responsible for deciding whom to baptize. It seems that we have made the decision regarding receiving and baptizing people an easy and convenient matter. Our basic problem is that we have not taken this matter seriously.

Many times we have simply accepted a person's word; however, the basic principle is that we must be serious when determining whether one should be received and baptized. If not, I am afraid that due to our negligence in this matter there will be confusion among us.

The matter of whom to receive and baptize has been a great controversy in the church from the time the first apostles passed away. Various Christian groups and sects all hold different views concerning this matter. Our principle in this matter is that we follow the Bible. Only those who believe should be baptized (Mark 16:16; Acts 8:12). This principle is correct, but how do we identify a person as a believing one, a saved one? This involves a number of difficulties. How can we determine whether or not a person has been saved? For him to be saved is one matter, but for us to determine whether he is saved is another matter. There is much room for interpretation. Perhaps one brother thinks that a man is not saved, but another thinks that he is saved. We may all agree to the principle of baptizing only those who are saved, but the difficulty lies in verifying the details. One brother may think that a certain person is saved, but I may think otherwise. Hence, there is much to consider when determining whether or not a person is saved. The definition of salvation among different believers also varies. Since there is variation in determining who is genuinely saved and in our understanding of what it means to be saved, there are always problems related to this matter. We do not have any problems in regard to principle, but we face difficulties in regard to carrying out the principle.

TWO ASPECTS OF SALVATION—
BELIEVING AND BEING BAPTIZED

According to our observation, for the past few years we have not had the wrong principle, but we have had an inaccurate understanding of salvation. We also were not accurate in determining who was saved; hence, certain problems arose.

What does it mean to be saved? Who is a saved one? What is the definition of salvation? To be fully saved requires first that we believe and second that we be baptized. Mark 16:16 says, "He who believes and is baptized shall be saved." The Bible does not say that he who believes and is saved shall be baptized but that he who believes and is baptized shall be saved. Hence, baptism is based on believing, not on being saved. To receive complete salvation, we must believe and be baptized. However, believing and being baptized are not two steps but can be considered as two "feet." Only when both feet step forward can they make a complete step. To believe and be baptized is one step, a complete step involving two "feet."

To receive salvation requires only one step: believing and being baptized. The Gospel of Mark says clearly that in order to receive God's salvation, one must believe and be baptized. However, this matter is not so simple. Strictly speaking, some portions of God's salvation can be received and obtained immediately through believing. In similar manner, when we enter a house, we must first put one foot forward. As soon as we put one foot forward, we have entered halfway. Once we bring our other foot forward, we are able to fully enter into the house. As soon as we believe, we receive a portion of God's salvation. It may not be complete, but it is at least partial salvation. Strictly speaking, baptism is based on believing, and baptism is also based on salvation. When a person believes, he truly receives a portion of salvation, and based upon this portion of salvation, he can be baptized. In another sense, baptism is not based upon salvation. A person is first baptized and then saved. It is true that a portion of salvation can be received only through baptism. Hence, being saved through believing, through baptism, and through believing and being baptized are three ways of describing the steps of salvation, and they do not conflict with one another.

WHAT MAN OBTAINS THROUGH BELIEVING

What is believing? What portion of salvation do we obtain through believing? Mark 16:16 says, "He who believes and is baptized shall be saved," whereas Romans 10:10 says, "With the heart there is believing unto righteousness, and with the mouth there is confession unto salvation." These verses indicate that a person does not need to be baptized in order to obtain righteousness. A person needs only to believe. Hence, when we baptize people, our basis is that they have believed. In other words, they must be those who have obtained righteousness.

John 3:36 says, "He who believes into the Son has eternal life; but he who disobeys the Son shall not see life." Baptism is not mentioned in this verse. It does not say that he who is baptized has eternal life; rather, it says that he who believes has eternal life. One who is baptized is one who has already believed. Believing precedes baptism. When a person believes in the Lord, he is first justified and then he obtains eternal life. To believe is to be justified and to obtain eternal life. To baptize someone based upon his believing is to baptize him based upon his receiving justification and eternal life.

Acts 10:43 says, "Through His name everyone who believes into Him will receive forgiveness of sins." Forgiveness of sins is the negative aspect of justification. Forgiveness of sins and justification are related and are actually one matter. This shows that one who believes receives forgiveness of sins, justification, and eternal life. Hence, the faith that qualifies a person to be baptized is a faith that brings him forgiveness of sins, justification, and eternal life.

BAPTISM BEING BASED UPON THE FAITH THAT ONE ALREADY HAS

When we contact someone, in order to determine whether he has the faith that qualifies him to be baptized, we must verify whether he has received forgiveness of sins, justification, and the life of God. If he has not received forgiveness of sins, justification, and the life of God, his "faith" cannot qualify him to be baptized. The faith that qualifies him to be baptized must result in his receiving forgiveness, justification, and God's life. Only such a faith makes it possible for a person to be saved; hence, only this faith can be the basis of baptism. This is the basic definition of faith. Some people's believing, however, is not according to God's revelation but according to their mind. When we contact such people, it is difficult to discern whether they are genuinely saved.

How can we know if a person has received forgiveness of sins, justification, and the life of God? In other words, how can we know if a person has faith? This is a crucial matter. Faith is in the psychological realm and is abstract. It is not like the two eyes and the nose on a person's face, which everyone can see and about which there is no doubt of their existence. However, faith is something abstract. Although people can speak of it confidently, no one can bring it out and physically show it to others. Hence, in order to help people clearly understand the matter, we must discover the manifestations of faith. In this sense, faith may be likened to electricity. Electricity for the most part is invisible, but it does have certain manifestations. As far as man's sight is concerned, electricity is invisible. It cannot be shown and is abstract. But as far as its practicality is concerned, it has certain manifestations.

When we see light shining from an electric lamp, hear sounds emitting from a radio, and smell aromas coming out of an oven, we know that there is electricity. Electricity is invisible, but according to its manifestations, we know that it exists. In the same way, faith is something that cannot be shown. Whether a person's faith is only mental or based on revelation, it is something that cannot be shown to people. Nevertheless, man can perceive the manifestations of faith. One of the manifestations of faith is the forgiveness of sins, another is justification, and yet another is the receiving of God's life. Nevertheless, how can we perceive these manifestations? For many years we have paid much attention to and emphasized one thing; that is, when we contact people, we should not neglect to sense their inward feeling. When we discuss the matter of baptism with people, we may have paid more attention to what they have spoken than to their inward feeling.

In order to determine whether a person has received forgiveness of sins, we must first sense whether he has an inward feeling concerning sins. When we converse with him, we need to sense whether he has any feeling concerning sins. Paying attention to what he says explicitly or how much he knows concerning the truth of salvation is not as important as touching his inmost feeling concerning sins. He must sense before the Lord that he has sins and that within him he has the enlightening of the Holy Spirit.

Sometimes I watched brothers converse with a person concerning baptism. After speaking with him for a long time, they were not clear whether he should be baptized. However, as I observed them, I became clear because his "accent" exposed him. If we want to know where a person is from, that is, whether he is from the South or North, we need him to speak only a few words. His accent will expose him. If I were to say that I am from southern China, few would believe me, because I speak with a northern accent. If I do not speak, even though a person may know that I am a Northerner, he would have no proof or evidence. As soon as I open my mouth and say that I am a Southerner, everyone will know that I am actually a Northerner. Despite what I say, my speaking, accent, and mannerisms will demonstrate that I am a Northerner.

Sometimes we may ask a person, "Do you know that you are sinful?" He may reply, "I am not sure what is sin, but in regard to the Lord I have been feeling uneasy for several days and nights." In the end, we may judge that because this person is unclear regarding sin, he is not qualified to be baptized.

This shows our spiritual blindness. We should not determine whether a person is ready to be baptized based on his words alone, that is, the explicit meaning of his words, but based on the spirit of his words. A person may tell us that he hates someone, but actually, we may know that he loves this person very much. Although he uses the word *hate,* the spirit behind his word is love. In school, government, or license examinations the only thing that matters is what is explicitly said. There is no regard for the real condition or spirit behind what is spoken. A correct answer is right, and an incorrect answer is wrong. There is no concern for whether a person is genuinely right or genuinely wrong.

When we talk with people regarding baptism, our goal should not be for them to meet a formal requirement. Hence, we do not need to monotonously ask them about their consciousness of sins. Once while I was involved in interviews for baptism in Foochow, a woman came who was a gospel friend. The first question I asked her was, "Have you consecrated yourself?" She said, "I am really sinful." Then I asked, "What will you do then?" She said, "I have no way. I come to take refuge in the Lord Jesus." Then I continued to ask her, "How can the Lord Jesus save you?" She replied, "I thank Him for dying for me on the cross." I further asked her, "Has He forgiven you of your sins?" She said, "I do not know. I only know that the Lord has died for me on the cross." At that point, I felt that there was no need to ask anything further and that it was proper to let her be baptized. She had been touched, contacted, and enlightened by the Holy Spirit. Hence, she needed to be baptized. Once she was baptized, she would be clear. This is what is meant by "he who believes and is baptized shall be saved" (Mark 16:16).

Many people have believed, but few are clear that they have been saved. They are not clear because they lack one thing—baptism. We cannot save people by baptizing them, but through baptism we can make them clear regarding their salvation. This is not a matter of doctrine. We cannot determine that a person is saved simply because he answers all our questions correctly. The most important matter to determine is whether he has contacted God and has been touched by God inwardly. This is a matter related to a person's inward feeling. All of us, especially the responsible brothers, must have a change in our understanding. We should not determine a person's readiness to be baptized based on his answering all of our questions correctly. Instead, we should look for indications or manifestations of his having been touched by the Holy Spirit. In other words, we have to see if the "electricity" has been transmitted into him. If he begins to give off "light," "sound," and "aroma," this is proof that inwardly he has been connected to the electricity.

Once we have confirmed that a person has been forgiven, has been justified, and has received life, we will be able to prove that he has the faith necessary for baptism. Sometimes we are made clear by speaking merely one sentence. We may not even have finished half a question, yet we become clear that the person to whom we are speaking has contacted God inwardly. Of course, at other times we may talk with a person for two hours but still not be able to figure out if God has contacted him. Proper discernment requires that we develop certain skills. When we receive people and have a conversation with them regarding baptism, our decision regarding whether to baptize them should be made by sensing whether they have been contacted by God inwardly, not by testing them concerning doctrines.

When we address the matter of forgiveness of sins, we should first touch a person's feeling concerning sins and then ask whether he has repented and confessed his sins before God. When we ask someone regarding prayer and confession, he may say that he has prayed and confessed his sins; nevertheless in his speaking, we may sense that he does not have much inward feeling regarding confession. A person may confess his sins, but he may not have much feeling. For example, in a play an actor may call another person "Daddy," but he does so without any feeling. However, when our children call us "Daddy," it is full of affection. When a stranger calls us daddy, other people can tell that he is a stranger. When our children call us daddy, others can also tell that they are our own children. The feeling is altogether different.

Someone may tell us that he has confessed his sins, but we should determine whether he has truly confessed his sins by touching the feeling behind his words, not by the words themselves. Hence, we should question him further, asking, "You have sins, and you have also confessed your sins, but how do you deal with your sins?" This will lead him to the cross. We should not try to verify merely whether he knows about the cross but whether he has truly experienced the cross and whether he has a relationship with the cross, the Lord Jesus, and the blood of the Lord Jesus. Let us consider the sister from Foochow, whom we mentioned previously. She did not know if her sins were forgiven, but the feeling and taste made it clear that she had a relationship with the crucified Savior. It is one thing to have the relationship; it is another thing to merely know about the relationship. What we care for is not the knowing but the relationship itself. Hence, we need to observe what a person's inward feeling is upon receiving the cross and to ask him how he feels concerning the Lord's death and his being forgiven by the Lord. Perhaps he would say that he does not know and is not that clear; nevertheless, we need to touch his inner feeling. He should feel grateful to the Lord, be full of thanksgiving, and have a peace within that is incomprehensible to him. His words may not be clear, but behind his words there should be a tangible reality.

For example, when we go to Yangmingshan, a national park in Taiwan, it is easily identifiable by its streams of water and the odor of sulfur, which is due to the water passing through sulfur deposits as it flows out of the ground. The odor is strong, and there is no room for imitation. Likewise, when a person speaks, something within is expressed, producing a kind of "flavor." When we hear a person's words, we should not only listen to the words that are spoken but should also sense the flavor that is brought forth through the words. Water is water, but some water carries the flavor of sulfur, some the flavor of a ditch, and some the flavor of a clear spring. Hence, the taste of the water is different because of the places through which the water flows.

Justification is a difficult experience to confirm. However, if a person has a clear experience of the forgiveness of sins, surely he is a justified person. In this sense, some can readily describe the feeling of justification. If you ask him, "Do you know that you are saved?" He would say, "I truly know that I am saved. Formerly I was one who opposed God and was at enmity with Him; whenever I thought of God, I was full of hatred. But now whenever God's name is mentioned, I feel joyful and sweet within." There is usually no need to ask such a person any further questions. However, to be cautious, we should ask him, "Do you have any feeling concerning sins? What is your realization concerning the Lord's dying on the cross for you?" Such questions will help us verify that he is not experiencing mere psychological excitement without touching the spiritual reality.

We have indeed met this kind of person before; although, he does not know the Lord Jesus adequately and is not clear about the cross, he repeatedly says that whenever he hears God's name, he is joyful within. Hence, to be cautious, we should still ask him a few more questions. Of course, we also need to take into account a person's environment and background. If a person has been coming to the meetings for several days and is clear concerning the truths regarding the Lord Jesus and the redemption of the cross, we should have the confidence not to ask him any further questions. However, if a stranger tells us that whenever he hears God's name he is joyful, we should ask him a few more questions from another angle in order to have a clear sense of where he is at. We should do this because we do not know his background or real condition. Hence, when we are confirming a person's justification, first, we need to touch his former condition toward God; second, we need to find out his knowledge of the cross; third, we need to sense his inward response in regard to his receiving of the cross. The principle is always the same.

When we are confirming the experiences of life, we should not use too many words or pay too much attention to the outward changes in a person's living; rather, we should pay attention to his inward change in life, as expressed by his psychological being and his inner feeling. He may tell us that formerly he was happy doing certain things, but now he is not happy when he does them. Previously, he did not like certain things, but now he likes them very much. As we listen to him describing these things, we need to touch what is behind his words, that is, his change in life and disposition. In the past, when he heard of God, he felt disgusted inwardly, but now whenever God is mentioned, he is joyful. This is clearly a change in disposition. In the past he was happy when he danced, but now without any apparent reason he feels miserable when he goes dancing. This is a change in life, not a change merely in behavior.

NEEDING TO TOUCH A PERSON'S INNER FEELING WHEN RECEIVING HIM

Like every other spiritual matter, the receiving of people is not so simple. When we receive people, the most crucial matter is to sense their inner feeling. Such feelings cannot be imitated. We must develop the ability to sense the feeling within others. Our problem is that we often have difficulty discerning people. Although some people have truly been saved, we fail to sense it and thus do not baptize them. Whereas others are not saved, yet we baptize them because we think that they are saved. This is not a matter of being loose or strict but a matter of being able to discern the spiritual reality within them.

Some brothers might suggest that we need to be strict in the matter of receiving people, lest some unsaved ones "sneak" in. However, if we are too strict, we will "squeeze out" those who are truly saved. As a result, some might suggest that we should be more lenient in order to avoid mishandling people. However, once we are lenient, more problems may arise. Hence, this is not a matter of being strict or lenient but of learning to discern the spiritual reality in others.

We must learn to sense what is behind a person's speaking. The brothers in the churches who are responsible for making decisions regarding whom to receive and baptize need to bear the responsibility to learn how to discern a person's inward feeling. They should absolutely not be loose in this matter. To not be loose means that those who bear the responsibility for making decisions regarding whom to baptize have developed a spiritual "nose" to discern a person's real condition. We may not be able to see or hear a man's inward condition, but we should be able to "smell" it. For example, a guest may come to your house. After sitting for a while, he may suddenly say to you, "There is a certain place which sells good sodas." If you then reply, "Yes, I have been there before," this shows that your "nose," your feeling, is not sensitive. If your feeling were sensitive, you would immediately serve him a beverage. Even if you do not have sodas, you should at least serve him some water.

Moreover, an opinionated and subjective person should never be involved in the matter of determining whom to receive. One who is responsible to determine whether or not a person can be received and baptized must exercise his spiritual "nose" and then exercise to be very objective. His attitude must be that regardless of how a certain person may be, he must objectively sense the person's inward spiritual reality before God. If we exercise in this way, our errors will be greatly reduced. If we consider the past, we will realize that most of our mistakes were made due to a lack of spiritual sense and objectiveness.

We must exercise much consideration when assigning a person to be responsible for the matter of receiving people. If the person assigned is not accurate, many unsaved ones will be brought into the church. The matter of determining whom to baptize should not be entrusted to others in a light way. Rather, because this matter is of much importance, we should be strict when choosing and examining those to whom we are considering to entrust it. If the person who makes the judgment is not accurate, the result will be unthinkable, and we will displease the Lord and delay His work. This is a solemn matter. It is not a matter of being loose or strict but a matter of discerning what is true or false.

I hope we will all see that in the church receiving people is a great and solemn matter. It can be likened to a big door, which, if not properly controlled, will allow many who have not been saved to be baptized and brought into the church and will cause many who are truly saved to be shut out. May the Lord have mercy on us so that all the churches may take the matter of receiving people seriously and solemnly. We should not be narrow-minded and closed; rather, we should without bias receive and acknowledge as brothers all those who are saved and who have inwardly contacted God. However, we must be very careful to not let any unsaved ones who have not contacted God enter the church. We must take this matter seriously. Otherwise, in the future more problems will arise in the church because there will be many who are not clearly saved among us. This will not only cause problems, but it is also a mistake before God and an offense to God. We must stress that it is not a matter of being loose or strict but a matter of whether our discernment is accurate or inaccurate.

CHAPTER EIGHT

FELLOWSHIP GIVEN IN A PRAYER MEETING CONCERNING THE FULL-TIME TRAINING

The Lord burdened us to spend some specific time to look to Him. If our body is able to make it, we will kneel down before the Lord and fast and pray for three mornings. During this training we have focused mostly on our homework and have rarely spent time together in prayer. We concentrate our efforts on homework and have little time and energy to pray to the Lord. Every time we pray, we should spend much time to have specific prayers before the Lord. We should consider prayer as our way to take care of business and do our work. The prayer meeting should not be an ordinary meeting. It is a time when we come together to do business before the Lord in prayer.

PRAYING FOR THE FULL-TIME TRAINING

Giving Thanks to the Lord for the Training

When we pray, I hope we will pay attention to four items: First, we should give thanks to the Lord. We need to thank Him for guiding us peacefully and smoothly through the training and for blessing us and being gracious to us in so many respects. Many of our brothers and sisters have participated in this training despite impossible situations. In all these situations the Lord has been gracious to us and brought us through step by step. Many of us, in terms of the capacity of our physical body, would have had no way to meet the various requirements of the training, but the Lord has brought us through. During the training we have been busy with many things, running here and there, yet the Lord has cared for us and sustained us in many ways. The Lord has also kept many of the families of the brothers and sisters from distracting matters. Of the approximately four hundred trainees, none of them has had any mishaps during this period of time. We thank the Lord for this.

Moreover, the Lord has also provided us with the most convenient environmental arrangement, materials, and personnel. We can say that we have had no lack, no problem, in terms of general affairs and financial matters. Thus, we have been able to concentrate all our effort and energy on the teaching materials. This has truly been a great blessing from the Lord. At the same time, we also thank Him for the speaking, messages, and materials He has given us.

Looking to the Lord for His Blessing on the Results of the Training

Second, we should look to the Lord concerning the training that we have received. We need to pray solemnly to the Lord to offer this training to Him, to give ourselves into His hand, and to ask for His blessing. We should not trust in anything except the Lord's blessing. No matter how much we do, without the Lord's blessing everything is in vain and empty. All that we have and do depends on the Lord's blessing. Hence, we look to the Lord to add His blessing to the training.

I hope that in the coming days we will see the result of this training manifested in each one of us year after year. Together we must look to the Lord for this training to produce ongoing results so that the words spoken in the training will gradually shine in our being to become part of our being and our practical experience. We also ask the Lord that in the coming years, whether it be two, three, or even four years, He will lead us to review these lessons so that we can experience the reality spoken of in them in our daily living and service and thereby supply His Body.

Asking the Lord for His Shining

Third, each one of us needs to kneel before the Lord and look to Him for His shining. During this time we should ask the Lord to shine on us and touch us regarding our personal condition, problems, and any matter that we have not been able to get through, escape, put aside, overcome, or deal with before Him. This is a heavy burden within. I hope that in the Lord's presence we can all be enlightened and touched by Him. Whether we have a problem with our character, with a spiritual matter, with our coordination, or with our work, we should ask the Lord to meet us in all these problems.

Looking to the Lord Corporately for the Church

Fourth, we need to look to the Lord corporately for His church. We should look to Him to show us how His church should advance. What does He want to accomplish on earth through the church? How should we follow the Lord? What function does the church carry out for the Lord on the earth? What does the Lord desire the church to carry out in this age? We must ask the Lord for His blessing and grace that the church would be well pleasing to Him on the earth, that whatever should be used would be used by Him, that whatever should be blessed would receive His blessing, that whatever should be released for the Lord's gospel would be released, that those who should fight for the Lord would fight for Him absolutely, and that those who should testify for the Lord would testify for Him faithfully. May the church be able to follow the Lord's leading and meet His need. May the church be blessed so that it does not lose His presence.

If the Lord so leads, we should all kneel down to pray. Whether we pray out loud one by one, pray silently, or pray out loud simultaneously depends on our sense from the Lord. In other words, this should not be fixed but should be free and spontaneous. Sometimes a certain atmosphere requires everyone to be quiet and pray one by one. Another time in a certain situation we may all need to be silent before the Lord. At yet another time every one of us may need to open our mouth simultaneously. Some might grieve and confess before the Lord, and others may offer thanks and praises before Him. Whatever the case, we should grant the Holy Spirit absolute liberty.

On the one hand, we need to give the Lord the liberty, but on the other hand, we need to fear the Lord. None of us should be unruly or loose before the Lord, and none should have his own activity or an intention to make a display of himself. We pray that the Lord would meet us in a strong way.

EXPERIENCING THE BREAKING

The Lord has been working among us and leading us throughout the years. Now many brothers and sisters have been brought to the point where they must pass through a crisis; that is, there is a problem within them that must be resolved. This problem is related to coordination, that is, to the work. The problem is that there are matters in us that still have not been broken. By the Lord's mercy, some saints have a fearful heart before the Lord. As a result, if they have an opinion, they dare not express it, and if they have something to say, they dare not voice it. This preserves a peaceful situation outwardly; however, the brothers and sisters experience no inward breaking.

Due to a lack of being broken in particular matters, the brothers and sisters seemingly do not have any problems, but actually they inwardly encounter real difficulties. These problems affect the coordination. Some have a feeling regarding certain matters within them, but they would not submit to or accept the feeling. Although they know that certain matters within them should be condemned, they are not determined to condemn these matters. Even though the saints know that these matters are natural, of the flesh, have been rejected by the Lord, and are what the Lord wants them to reject, few have the intention or determination to reject these matters. This is our human weakness, our human condition.

Many times the Lord has given us a feeling that we should deal with a certain matter, but for some reason, our feeling toward the matter is slothful and inadequate, and our spirit is reluctant to move. It seems that our mind knows that the matter should be judged and condemned, but our spirit cannot rise up, and our entire being cannot move. It is true that we have been enlightened, but within us there is no response to the shining and no ability to move. Hence, when people contact us, they sense that we are dull and closed both to them and to the Lord. Because we have a heart that fears the Lord, we dare not blame the brothers or have any disharmony with them, yet inwardly we are full of reservations.

Today many brothers and sisters among us in local churches are in this condition. This does not mean that they have backslidden spiritually; rather, they have come to a certain stage in their spiritual journey, a stage through which we all must pass. When we first begin to serve the Lord, there is a period of excitement. During this time, it is difficult for us to discover our problems, because we are immature and stay in the excitement of our emotion. In this time of excitement, it is difficult to discover the natural hindrances in us. Under the Lord's leading, however, we pass through a long process and spontaneously enter into another stage. At this time, the excitement and tide of our feelings subside. We then discover that within us there remains something that hinders us from coordinating with the brothers, something quite strong, something as big and hard as the rocks by the seashore, that is, our natural man, our flesh, and the self.

We have been shown mercy and have learned the lesson of fearing God; hence, even though we know that we cannot coordinate with the brothers, we do not dare to let ourselves, our flesh, become loose. Outwardly, it may seem that something has changed, but inwardly, something remains which causes us to be in the self, to be unable to coordinate with the brothers, and to be closed to them and to the Lord. Some people remain in this condition for many years. We human beings are strange. When it comes to the matter of submission, we are not clear-cut and decisive. Even when we have had some deep inward experiences, we are still hesitant in the matter of submission. Some hesitate for a period of a year or two, perhaps even for three or four years. Many times we know clearly that there is a certain matter in which we need to submit; nevertheless, even though the feeling to submit is in us, we do not submit.

Today in many churches a number of brothers and sisters are inwardly dull and dead, without the freshness and livingness of life. This is mainly because they are not willing to submit and be broken. They do not quarrel or argue with others and do not criticize or condemn others; however, if we have a keen sense in our spirit, we touch a pile of hard rocks within them. The tide comes and goes, but the pile of rocks stands firm and stable. Although the Lord has shined on them many times, and their inner sense condemns the same matters again and again, submission is difficult for such people.

We are often slothful and stingy in the matter of submission; thus, we truly need more of the Lord's grace and mercy. We may see our natural man and know our self, but we may have no power to overcome them. We have no way to deal with our natural man, and we have no power to respond to the Lord's demands in us. We must ask the Lord to have mercy on us and to add grace to us so that by Him we can deal with and solve this problem.

BEING DESPERATE BEFORE THE LORD TO WRESTLE WITH HIM

A person who is unwilling to submit to the Lord's shining cannot be helped by anyone. We may pray for him, speak to him, or fellowship with him, but time after time we will realize that his problem remains. When we fellowship with him, it seems as if he has received some help, but afterward he will remain in the same condition and still be reluctant to submit. No one can help him. He himself must bear some responsibility to overcome his being slothful and "stingy." At least he should be like Jacob, who wrestled with the Lord at the ford of the Jabbok (Gen. 32:22-32).

Many of us realize that in our service, coordination, and spiritual life, we have come to a point where we cannot go further. Although outwardly speaking, nothing has gone wrong, there is no apparent dispute, and it seems as if nothing is amiss, yet inwardly we may be clear that we, like Jacob, have come to the ford of the Jabbok. On that day Jacob made a determination to wrestle with God, but our problem is that we lack the resolve to wrestle. We are slothful both in spirit and in feeling. May the Lord have mercy on us.

In this training there is nothing to offer that causes excitement. The more one gains the Lord and touches the Lord's word inwardly, the more a killing element operates in him to put him to death. In other words, this training is held not in "spring" but in "winter." On our part, we need to be put to death again and again. Perhaps when some brothers go back to their localities after the training, they will not be able to speak a message or even open their mouths to pray in the meetings. This is because a problem still remains in them. The problem has always been there, but it was not exposed. Through the training, however, the problem has been exposed. The more a person's problem is exposed, the weaker he becomes until eventually he is not able to rise up inwardly. This causes him to not be able to break through. He cannot break through in the work, in the ministry of the word, in coordination, or in the spiritual life. This is the ford of the Jabbok.

We should not be discouraged. We need to look to the Lord for His mercy that we, like Jacob, will become so desperate before the Lord that we will wrestle with Him. We can discuss our weakness with the Lord, saying, "Lord, even though I am not desperate, I should not be slothful. What should I do with my slothful attitude?" If we cannot rise up inwardly, we need to discuss this with the Lord. When we approach the Lord in this way, we should not be too concerned about the price we need to pay. To be concerned about the price is a big distraction. We should simply tell the Lord that we want to solve our problem and discuss with Him what we should do about the slothfulness in our being and what we should do when our spirit cannot rise up. We need to pray to the Lord in this way.

We should never ignore our inward sense of condemnation, and we should never let a feeling of condemnation go. We should accept every feeling of condemnation and not make excuses for ourselves. To excuse ourselves is to be loose with ourselves, to let ourselves go. Feeling condemned stops and restricts us, whereas excusing ourselves frees us. The extent to which we try to excuse away our inner sense of condemnation is the extent to which we miss out on grace, whereas the more we accept the condemnation, the more grace we will receive.

Our condition before the Lord very much affects the church. Whether the church of God will have a free way to advance depends on whether we can get through this crisis. If our inward problem is resolved, the church of God will have a way to progress. Otherwise, I do not know how long the Lord will be delayed before the church has a way to advance. I implore all the brothers and sisters, especially the responsible ones in the churches, to receive this word. May the Lord have mercy on us.

About the Author

Witness Lee was born in 1905 in northern China and raised in a Christian family. At age 19 he was fully captured for Christ and immediately consecrated himself to preach the gospel for the rest of his life. Early in his service, he met Watchman Nee, a renowned preacher, teacher, and writer. Witness Lee labored together with Watchman Nee under his direction. In 1934 Watchman Nee entrusted Witness Lee with the responsibility for his publication operation, called the Shanghai Gospel Bookroom.

Prior to the Communist takeover in 1949, Witness Lee was sent by Watchman Nee and his other co-workers to Taiwan to ensure that the things delivered to them by the Lord would not be lost. Watchman Nee instructed Witness Lee to continue the former's publishing operation abroad as the Taiwan Gospel Bookroom, which has been publicly recognized as the publisher of Watchman Nee's works outside China. Witness Lee's work in Taiwan manifested the Lord's abundant blessing. From a mere 350 believers, newly fled from the mainland, the churches in Taiwan grew to 20,000 in five years.

In 1962 Witness Lee felt led of the Lord to come to the United States, settling in California. During his 35 years of service in the U.S., he ministered in weekly meetings and weekend conferences, delivering several thousand spoken messages. Much of his speaking has since been published as over 400 titles. Many of these have been translated into over fourteen languages. He gave his last public conference in February 1997 at the age of 91.

He leaves behind a prolific presentation of the truth in the Bible. His major work, *Life-study of the Bible,* comprises over 25,000 pages of commentary on every book of the Bible from the perspective of the believers' enjoyment and experience of God's divine life in Christ through the Holy Spirit. Witness Lee was the chief editor of a new translation of the New Testament into Chinese called the Recovery Version and directed the translation of the same into English. The Recovery Version also appears in a number of other languages. He provided an extensive body of footnotes, outlines, and spiritual cross references. A radio broadcast of his messages can be heard on Christian radio stations in the United States. In 1965 Witness Lee founded Living Stream Ministry, a non-profit corporation, located in Anaheim, California, which officially presents his and Watchman Nee's ministry.

Witness Lee's ministry emphasizes the experience of Christ as life and the practical oneness of the believers as the Body of Christ. Stressing the importance of attending to both these matters, he led the churches under his care to grow in Christian life and function. He was unbending in his conviction that God's goal is not narrow sectarianism but the Body of Christ. In time, believers began to meet simply as the church in their localities in response to this conviction. In recent years a number of new churches have been raised up in Russia and in many eastern European countries.

OTHER BOOKS PUBLISHED BY
Living Stream Ministry

Titles by Witness Lee:

Abraham—Called by God	0-7363-0359-6
The Experience of Life	0-87083-417-7
The Knowledge of Life	0-87083-419-3
The Tree of Life	0-87083-300-6
The Economy of God	0-87083-415-0
The Divine Economy	0-87083-268-9
God's New Testament Economy	0-87083-199-2
The World Situation and God's Move	0-87083-092-9
Christ vs. Religion	0-87083-010-4
The All-inclusive Christ	0-87083-020-1
Gospel Outlines	0-87083-039-2
Character	0-87083-322-7
The Secret of Experiencing Christ	0-87083-227-1
The Life and Way for the Practice of the Church Life	0-87083-785-0
The Basic Revelation in the Holy Scriptures	0-87083-105-4
The Crucial Revelation of Life in the Scriptures	0-87083-372-3
The Spirit with Our Spirit	0-87083-798-2
Christ as the Reality	0-87083-047-3
The Central Line of the Divine Revelation	0-87083-960-8
The Full Knowledge of the Word of God	0-87083-289-1
Watchman Nee—A Seer of the Divine Revelation ...	0-87083-625-0

Titles by Watchman Nee:

How to Study the Bible	0-7363-0407-X
God's Overcomers	0-7363-0433-9
The New Covenant	0-7363-0088-0
The Spiritual Man 3 volumes	0-7363-0269-7
Authority and Submission	0-7363-0185-2
The Overcoming Life	1-57593-817-0
The Glorious Church	0-87083-745-1
The Prayer Ministry of the Church	0-87083-860-1
The Breaking of the Outer Man and the Release ...	1-57593-955-X
The Mystery of Christ	1-57593-954-1
The God of Abraham, Isaac, and Jacob	0-87083-932-2
The Song of Songs	0-87083-872-5
The Gospel of God 2 volumes	1-57593-953-3
The Normal Christian Church Life	0-87083-027-9
The Character of the Lord's Worker	1-57593-322-5
The Normal Christian Faith	0-87083-748-6
Watchman Nee's Testimony	0-87083-051-1

Available at
Christian bookstores, or contact Living Stream Ministry
2431 W. La Palma Ave. • Anaheim, CA 92801
1-800-549-5164 • www.livingstream.com